Handbook of Selected Court Cases

to accompany

West's American Government

West Publishing Company
St. Paul•New York•Los Angeles•San Francisco

WEST'S COMMITMENT TO THE ENVIRONMENT

In 1906, West Publishing Company began recycling materials left over from the production of books. This began a tradition of efficient and responsible use of resources. Today, up to 95% of our legal books and 70% of our college texts are printed on recycled, acid-free stock. West also recycles nearly 22 million pounds of scrap paper annually—the equivalent of 181,717 trees. Since the 1960s, West has devised ways to capture and recycle waste inks, solvents, oils, and vapors created in the printing process. We also recycle plastics of all kinds, wood, glass, corrugated cardboard, and batteries, and have eliminated the use of styrofoam book packaging. We at West are proud of the longevity and the scope of our commitment to our environment.

Production, Prepress, Printing and Binding by West Publishing Company.

610 Opperman Drive
P.O. Box 64526
St. Paul, MN 55164–0526

Printed in the United States of America
00 99 98 97 96 95 94 93 8 7 6 5 4 3 2 1 0

ISBN 0–314–01097–1

Table of Contents

Preface

This booklet contains original source material pulled from important Supreme Court decisions as reported by West Publishing Company's WESTLAW Division. In order to make these case excerpts more understandable, we have broken them up into five parts.

- **The Case Citation**—This full citation includes the date the case was argued before the Supreme Court and the date that the Supreme Court decided the case.

- **Introduction**—This introduction is in our words and simply gives you and your students a brief idea of what the case involves.

- **WESTLAW Summary**—This summary is taken directly from WESTLAW, the computerized case reporting service of West Publishing Company. Of course, much of the language here is quite "legalese," but it does give a flavor of how the legal community would summarize the case under study.

- **Case Excerpts**—These are the actual words of the court. They are preceded by the name of the justice who rendered the Supreme Court decision. Of course, these are excerpts only, for many of these cases are extremely long.

- **Decision**—The actual decision, in the words of the court, is presented.

To help you understand case citations and other aspects of these important Supreme Court cases, we present below a summary of relevant information about court cases.

Federal Court Decisions

Federal trial court decisions are published unofficially in West's *Federal Supplement* (F.Supp.), and opinions from the circuit courts of appeals are reported unofficially in West's *Federal Reporter* (F. or F.2d, where 2d refers to Second Series). Cases concerning federal bankruptcy law are published unofficially in West's *Bankruptcy Reporter* (Bankr.). Opinions from the

United States Supreme Court are reported in the *United States Reports* (U.S.), West's *Supreme Court Reporter* (S.Ct.), the *Lawyers' Edition of the Supreme Court Reports* (L.Ed. or L.Ed.2d), and other publications.

The *United States Reports* is the official edition of all decisions of the United States Supreme Court for which there are written opinions. Published by the federal government, the series includes reports of Supreme Court cases dating from the August term of 1791, although originally many of the decisions were not reported in the early volumes.

West's *Supreme Court Reporter* is an unofficial edition dating from the Court's term in October 1882. Preceding each of its case reports are a summary of the case and *headnotes* (brief editorial statements of the law involved in the case, numbered to correspond to numbers in the report). The headnotes are also given classification numbers that serve to cross-reference each headnote to other headnotes on similar points throughout the National Reporter System and other West publications to facilitate research of all relevant cases on a given point.

The Lawyers Cooperative Publishing Company of Rochester, New York, publishes the *Lawyers' Edition of the Supreme Court Reports,* which is an unofficial edition of the entire series of the Supreme Court reports and contains many of the decisions not reported in the early official volumes. Also, among other editorial features, the *Lawyers' Edition,* in its second series, precedes the report of each case with a full summary, includes excerpts from briefs of counsel, and discusses in detail selected cases of special interest to the legal profession.

A Sample Case Citation

The first case in this handbook is *Afroyim v. Rusk.* Its full case citation is:

Beys **AFROYIM**
v.
Dean **RUSK**
387 U.S. 253, 87 S.Ct. 1660, 18 L.Ed.2d 757.

In other words, it lists three separate parallel citations:

387 U.S. 253 means that this case can be found in volume 387 of the *United States Reports*, the official edition of the decisions of the United States Supreme Court. The case starts on page 253.

87 S.Ct. 1660 is the citation from West's *Supreme Court Reporter.* This case can be found in volume 87 starting on page 1660.

18 L.Ed.2d 757 is a citation for the Second Series of the *Lawyers' Edition of the Supreme Court Reports.* This case is found in volume 18 starting on page 757.

CASE TITLES

In the title of a case, such as *Afroyim v. Rusk,* the *v.* or *vs.* stands for versus, which means against. (This is also called the *style* of the case, or the names of the parties in the lawsuit.) In the trial court, Afroyim was the plaintiff—the person who filed the suit. Rusk was the defendant. If the case is appealed, however, the appellate court will sometimes place the name of the party appealing the decision first, so that the case may be called *Rusk v. Afroyim.* Because some appellate courts retain the trial court order of names, it is often impossible to distinguish the plaintiff from the defendant in the title of a reported appellate court decision. The researcher must carefully read the facts of each case in order to identify each party. Otherwise, the discussion by the appellate court will be difficult to understand.

TERMINOLOGY

The following terms and phrases are frequently encountered in court opinions and legal publications. Because it is important to understand what is meant by these terms and phrases, we define and discuss them here.

Decisions and Opinions Most decisions reached by reviewing, or appellate, courts are explained in writing. A decision, or opinion, contains the court's reasons for its decision, the rules of law that apply, and the judgment. There are four possible types of written opinions for any particular case decided by an appellate court. When all judges or justices unanimously agree on an opinion, the opinion is written for the entire court and can be deemed a **unanimous opinion.** When there is not a unanimous opinion, a **majority opinion** is written, outlining the views of the majority of the judges or justices deciding the case. Often a judge or justice who feels strongly about making or emphasizing a point that was not made or emphasized in the unanimous or majority opinion will write a **concurring opinion.** That means the judge or justice agrees (concurs) with the judgment given in the unanimous or majority opinion, but for different reasons. In other than unanimous opinions, a **dissenting opinion** is usually written by a judge or justice who does not agree with the majority. The dissenting opinion is important because it may form the basis of the arguments used years later in overruling the precedential majority opinion.

Judges and Justices The terms *judge* and *justice* are usually synonymous and represent two designations given to judges in various courts. All members of the United States Supreme Court, for example, are referred to as justices. And justice is the formal title usually given to judges of appellate courts, although this is not always the case. In New York, a justice is a trial judge of the trial court (which is called the Supreme Court), and a member of the Court of Appeals (the state's highest court) is called a judge. The term *justice* is commonly abbreviated to J., and *justices* to JJ. A Supreme Court case might refer to Justice Kennedy as Kennedy, J., or to Chief Justice Rehnquist as Rehnquist, C.J.

Appellants and Appellees The **appellant** is the party who appeals a case to another court or jurisdiction from the court or jurisdiction in which the case was originally brought. Sometimes, an appellant who appeals from a judgment is referred to as the **petitioner.** The **appellee** is the party against whom the appeal is taken. Sometimes, an appellee is referred to as the **respondent.**

Beys **AFROYIM**
v.
Dean **RUSK**
387 U.S. 253, 87 S.Ct. 1660, 18 L.Ed.2d 757.
Argued Feb. 20, 1967.
Decided May 29, 1967.

Introduction

A civil rights/citizenship case in which the Court ruled that all citizens have "a constitutional right to remain a citizen in a free country unless [they] voluntarily relinquish that citizenship." Part of the Nationality Act of 1940 was declared unconstitutional because it provided for the automatic expatriation of any American citizen who voted in a foreign election.

WESTLAW Summary

Action for declaratory judgment to test constitutionality of involuntary expatriation statute. The United States District Court for the Southern District of New York granted summary judgment for defendant, and plaintiff appealed. The United States Court of Appeals for the Second Circuit affirmed, and plaintiff obtained certiorari. The Supreme Court, Mr. Justice Black, held that under Fourteenth Amendment, government had no power to rob citizen of his citizenship under statute providing that citizen should lose his citizenship for voting in political election in a foreign state.

Case Excerpts

Mr. Justice BLACK delivered the opinion of the Court.

Petitioner, born in Poland in 1893, immigrated to this country in 1912 and became a naturalized American citizen in 1926. He went to Israel in 1950, and in 1951 he voluntarily voted in an election for the Israeli Knesset, the legislative body of Israel. In 1960, when he applied for renewal of his United States passport, the Department of State refused to grant it on the sole ground that he had lost his American citizenship by virtue of s 401(e) of the Nationality Act of 1940 which provides that a United States citizen shall "lose' his citizenship if he votes "in a political election in a foreign state.' Petitioner then brought this declaratory judgment action in federal district court alleging that s 401(e) violates both the Due Process Clause of the Fifth Amendment and s 1, cl. 1, of the Fourteenth Amendment which grants American citizenship to persons like petitioner. Because neither the Fourteenth Amendment nor any other provision of the Constitution expressly grants Congress the power to take away that citizenship once it has been acquired, petitioner contended that the only way he could lose his citizenship was by his own voluntary renunciation of it. Since the Government took the position that s 401(e) empowers it to terminate citizenship without the citizen's voluntary renunciation, petitioner argued that this section is prohibited by the Constitution. The District Court and the Court of Appeals, rejecting this argument, held that Congress has constitutional authority forcibly to take away citizenship for voting in a foreign country based on its implied power to regulate foreign affairs. Consequently, petitioner was held to have lost his American citizenship regardless of his intention not to give it up. * * *

* * * *

The fundamental issue before this Court here, as it was in Perez, is whether Congress can consistently with the Fourteenth Amendment enact a law stripping an American of his citizenship which he has never voluntarily renounced or given up. * * *

First we reject the idea * * * that, aside from the Fourteenth Amendment, Congress has any general power, express or implied, to take away an American citizen's citizenship without his assent. This power cannot * * * be sustained as an implied attribute of sovereignty possessed by all nations. Other nations are governed by their own constitutions, if any, and we can draw no support from theirs. In our country the people are sovereign and the Government cannot sever its relationship to the people by taking away their citizenship. Our Constitution governs us and we must never forget that our Constitution limits the Government to those powers specifically granted or those that are necessary and proper to carry out the specifically granted ones. The Constitution of course, grants Congress no express power to strip people of their citizenship, whether in the exercise of the implied power to regulate foreign affairs or in the exercise of any specifically granted power. And even before the adoption of the Fourteenth Amendment, views were expressed in Congress and by this Court that under the Constitution the Government was granted no power, even under its express power to pass a uniform rule of naturalization, to determine what conduct should and should not result in the loss of citizenship. * * *

* * * *

* * * [A]ny doubt as to whether prior to the passage of the Fourteenth Amendment Congress had the power to deprive a person against his will of citizenship once obtained should have been removed by the unequivocal terms of the Amendment itself. It provides its own constitutional rule in language calculated completely to control the status of citizenship: "All persons born or naturalized in the United States * * * are citizens of the United States * * *.' There is no indication in these words of a fleeting citizenship, good at the moment it is acquired but subject to destruction by the Government at any time. Rather the Amendment can most reasonably be read as defining a citizenship which a citizen keeps unless he voluntarily relinquishes it. Once acquired, this Fourteenth Amendment citizenship was not to be shifted, canceled, or diluted at the will of the Federal Government, the States, or any other governmental unit.

* * * *

* * * To uphold Congress' power to take away a man's citizenship because he voted in a foreign election in violation of s 401(e) would be equivalent to holding that Congress has the power to "abridge,' "affect,' "restrict the effect of,' and "take * * * away' citizenship. Because the Fourteenth Amendment prevents Congress from doing any of these things, * * * the Government is without power to rob a citizen of his citizenship under s 401(e).

Because the legislative history of the Fourteenth Amendment and of the expatriation proposals which preceded and followed it, like most other legislative history, contains many statements from which conflicting inferences can be drawn, our holding might be unwarranted if it rested entirely or principally upon that legislative history. But it does not. Our holding we think is the only one that can stand in view of the language and the purpose of the Fourteenth Amendment, and our construction of that Amendment, we believe, comports * * * with the principles of liberty and equal justice to all that the entire Fourteenth Amendment was adopted to guarantee. Citizenship is no light trifle to be jeopardized any moment Congress decides to do so under the name of one of its general or implied grants of power. In some instances, loss of citizenship can mean that a man is left without the protection of citizenship in any country in the world-as a man without a country. Citizenship in this Nation is a part of a cooperative affair. Its citizenry is the country and the country is its citizenry. The very nature of our free government makes it completely incongruous to have a rule of law under which a group of citizens temporarily in office can deprive another group of citizens of their citizenship. We hold that the Fourteenth Amendment was designed to, and does, protect every citizen of this Nation against a congressional forcible destruction of his citizenship, whatever his creed, color, or race. Our holding does no more than to give to this citizen that which is his own, a constitutional right to remain a citizen in a free country unless he voluntarily relinquishes that citizenship.

Decision

The judgment is reversed.

Charles W. **BAKER** et al.
v.
Joe C. **CARR** et al.
369 U.S. 186, 82 S.Ct. 691, 7 L.Ed.2d 663
Reargued Oct. 9, 1961.
Decided March 26, 1962.

Introduction

A Fourteenth Amendment/apportionment case in which the Court ruled that state legislatures had to be apportioned to provide equal protection under the law.

WESTLAW Summary

Action under the civil rights statute, by qualified voters of certain counties of Tennessee for a declaration that a state apportionment statute was an unconstitutional deprivation of equal protection of the laws, for an injunction, and other relief. A three-judge District Court, for the Middle District of Tennessee, entered an order dismissing the complaint, and plaintiffs appealed. The Supreme Court, Mr. Justice Brennan, held that complaint containing allegations that a state statute effected an apportionment that deprived plaintiffs of equal protection of the laws in violation of the Fourteenth Amendment presented a justiciable constitutional cause of action, and the right asserted was within reach of judicial protection under the Fourteenth Amendment, and did not present a nonjusticiable political question.

Case Excerpts

Mr. Justice BRENNAN delivered the opinion of the Court.

This civil action was brought * * * to redress the alleged deprivation of federal constitutional rights. The complaint, alleging that by means of a 1901 statute of Tennessee apportioning the members of the General Assembly among the State's 95 counties, "these plaintiffs and others similarly situated, are denied the equal protection of the laws accorded them by the Fourteenth Amendment to the Constitution of the United States by virtue of the debasement of their votes,' was dismissed by a three-judge court convened * * * in the Middle District of Tennessee. The court held that it lacked jurisdiction of the subject matter and also that no claim was stated upon which relief could be granted. We noted probable jurisdiction of the appeal. We hold that the dismissal was error, and remand the cause to the District Court for trial and further proceedings consistent with this opinion.

* * * *

* * * Tennessee's standard for allocating legislative representation among her counties is the total number of qualified voters resident in the respective counties, subject only to minor qualifications. * * * In 1901 the General Assembly abandoned separate enumeration in favor of reliance upon the Federal Census and passed the Apportionment Act here in controversy. In the more than 60 years since that action, all proposals in both Houses of the General Assembly for reapportionment have failed to pass.

* * * Indeed, the complaint alleges that the 1901 statute, even as of the time of its passage, "made no apportionment of Representatives and Senators in accordance with the constitutional formula * * *, but instead arbitrarily and capriciously apportioned representatives in the Senate and House without reference * * * to any logical or reasonable formula whatever.' * * * [The plaintiffs] seek a declaration that the 1901 statute is unconstitutional and an injunction restraining the appellees from acting to conduct any further elections under it.

JURISDICTION OF THE SUBJECT MATTER.

The District Court was uncertain whether our cases withholding federal judicial relief rested upon a lack of federal jurisdiction or upon the inappropriateness of the subject matter for judicial consideration-what we have designated "nonjusticiability.' The distinction between the two grounds is significant. In the instance of nonjusticiability, consideration of the cause is not wholly and immediately foreclosed; rather, the Court's inquiry necessarily proceeds to the point of deciding whether the duty asserted can be judicially identified and its breach ju-

dicially determined, and whether protection for the right asserted can be judicially molded. In the instance of lack of jurisdiction the cause either does not "arise under' the Federal Constitution, laws or treaties (or fall within one of the other enumerated categories of Art. III, s 2), or is not a "case or controversy' within the meaning of that section; or the cause is not one described by any jurisdictional statute. Our conclusion that this cause presents no nonjusticiable "political question' settles the only possible doubt that it is a case or controversy. Under the present heading of "Jurisdiction of the Subject Matter' we hold only that the matter set forth in the complaint does arise under the Constitution.
* * *

STANDING.

* * * *

These appellants seek relief in order to protect or vindicate an interest of their own, and of those similarly situated. Their constitutional claim is, in substance, that the 1901 statute constitutes arbitrary and capricious state action, offensive to the Fourteenth Amendment in its irrational disregard of the standard of apportionment prescribed by the State's Constitution or of any standard, effecting a gross disproportion of representation to voting population. The injury which appellants assert is that this classification disfavors the voters in the counties in which they reside, placing them in a position of constitutionally unjustifiable inequality vis-a -vis voters in irrationally favored counties.
* * *

JUSTICIABILITY.

We have said that "In determining whether a question falls within (the political question) category, the appropriateness under our system of government of attributing finality to the action of the political departments and also the lack of satisfactory criteria for a judicial determination are dominant considerations.' [citation omitted] The nonjusticiability of a political question is primarily a function of the separation of powers. Much confusion results from the capacity of the "political question' label to obscure the need for case-by-case inquiry. Deciding whether a matter has in any measure been committed by the Constitution to another branch of government, or whether the action of that branch exceeds whatever authority has been committed, is itself a delicate exercise in constitutional interpretation, and is a responsibility of this Court as ultimate interpreter of the Constitution.

* * * *

It is apparent that several formulations which vary slightly according to the settings in which the questions arise may describe a political question, although each has one or more elements which identify it as essentially a function of the separation of powers. Prominent on the surface of any case held to involve a political question is found a textually demonstrable constitutional commitment of the issue to a coordinate political department; or a lack of judicially discoverable and manageable standards for resolving it; or the impossibility of deciding without an initial policy determination of a kind clearly for nonjudicial discretion; or the impossibility of a court's undertaking independent resolution without expressing lack of the respect due coordinate branches of government; or an unusual need for unquestioning adherence to a political decision already made; or the potentiality of embarrassment from multifarious pronouncements by various departments on one question.

Unless one of these formulations is inextricable from the case at bar, there should be no dismissal for non-justiciability on the ground of a political question's presence. The doctrine of which we treat is one of "political questions,' not one of "political cases.' The courts cannot reject as "no law suit' a bona fide controversy as to whether some action denominated "political' exceeds constitutional authority. The cases we have reviewed show the necessity for discriminating inquiry into the precise facts and posture of the particular case, and the impossibility of resolution by any semantic cataloguing.

* * * *

We conclude then that the nonjusticiability of claims resting on the Guaranty Clause which arises from their embodiment of questions that were thought "political,' can have no bearing upon the justiciability of the equal protection claim presented in this case. Finally, we emphasize that it is the involvement in Guaranty Clause claims of the elements thought to define "political questions,' and no other feature, which could render them nonjusticiable. Specifically, we have said that such claims are not held nonjusticiable because they touch matters of state governmental organization.

* * * *

We conclude that the complaint's allegations of a denial of equal protection present a justiciable constitutional cause of action upon which appellants are entitled to a trial and a decision. The right asserted is within the reach of judicial protection under the Fourteenth Amendment.

Decision

The judgment of the District Court is reversed and the cause is remanded for further proceedings consistent with this opinion.

Jeffrey Cole **BIGELOW**
v.
Commonwealth of **VIRGINIA.**
421 U.S. 809, 95 S.Ct. 2222, 44 L.Ed. 600
Argued Dec. 18, 1974.
Decided June 16, 1975.

Introduction

A freedom of speech/advertising case involving so-called commercial speech in which the Court held that the state cannot prohibit newspaper advertising of abortion services.

WESTLAW Summary

The editor of weekly Virginia newspaper was convicted before the Circuit Court, Albemarle County, of violating a Virginia statute making it a misdemeanor, by the sale or circulation of any publication, to encourage or prompt the procuring of an abortion. The Virginia Supreme Court affirmed, and defendant appealed. The United States Supreme Court vacated and remanded. On reconsideration, the Virginia Supreme Court affirmed, and defendant appealed. The Supreme Court held that speech is not stripped of First Amendment protection merely because it appears in form of a paid commercial advertisement * * * and that statute as applied to the editor infringed constitutionally protected speech.

Case Excerpts

Mr. Justice BLACKMUN delivered the opinion of the Court.

An advertisement carried in appellant's newspaper led to his conviction for a violation of a Virginia statute that made it a misdemeanor, by the sale or circulation of any publication, to encourage or prompt the procuring of an abortion. The issue here is whether the editor-appellant's First Amendment rights were unconstitutionally abridged by the statute. The First Amendment, of course, is applicable to the States through the Fourteenth Amendment.

* * * *

The central assumption made by the Supreme Court of Virginia was that the First Amendment guarantees of speech and press are inapplicable to paid commercial advertisements. Our cases, however, clearly establish that speech is not stripped of First Amendment protection merely because it appears in that form. * * *

The fact that the particular advertisement in appellant's newspaper had commercial aspects or reflected the advertiser's commercial interests did not negate all First Amendment guarantees. * * *

* * * The advertisement published in appellant's newspaper did more than simply propose a commercial transaction. It contained factual material of clear "public interest.' Portions of its message, most prominently the lines, "Abortions are now legal in New York. There are no residency requirements,' involve the exercise of the freedom of communicating information and disseminating opinion.

Viewed in its entirety, the advertisement conveyed information of potential interest and value to a diverse audience-not only to readers possibly in need of the services offered, but also to those with a general curiosity about, or genuine interest in, the subject matter or the law of another State and its development, and to readers seeking reform in Virginia. The mere existence of the Women's Pavilion in New York City, with the possibility of its being typical of other organizations there, and the availability of the services offered, were not unnewsworthy. Also, the activity advertised pertained to constitutional interests. Thus, in this case, appellant's First Amendment interests coincided with the constitutional interests of the general public.

Moreover, the placement services advertised in appellant's newspaper were legally provided in New York at that time. The Virginia Legislature could not have regulated the advertiser's activity in New York, and obviously could not have proscribed the activity in that State. Neither could Virginia prevent its residents from traveling to New York to obtain those services or, as the State conceded, prosecute them for going there. Virginia possessed no authority to regulate the services provided in New York-the skills and credentials of the New York physicians and of the New York professionals who assisted them, the standards of the New York hospitals and clinics to which patients were referred, or the practices and charges of the New York referral services.

A State does not acquire power or supervision over the internal affairs of another State merely because the welfare and health of its own citizens may be affected when they travel to that State. It may seek to disseminate information so as to enable its citizens to make better informed decisions when they leave. But it may not, under the guise of exercising internal police powers, bar a citizen of another State from disseminating information about an activity that is legal in that State.

We conclude, therefore, that the Virginia courts erred in their assumptions that advertising, as such, was entitled to no First Amendment protection and that appellant Bigelow had no legitimate First Amendment interest. We need not decide in this case the precise extent to which the First Amendment permits regulation of advertising that is related to activities the State may legitimately regulate or even prohibit.

Advertising, like all public expression, may be subject to reasonable regulation that serves a legitimate public interest. To the extent that commercial activity is subject to regulation, the relationship of speech to that activity may be one factor, among others, to be considered in weighing the First Amendment interest against the governmental interest alleged. Advertising is not thereby stripped of all First Amendment protection. The relationship of speech to the marketplace of products or of services does not make it valueless in the marketplace of ideas.

* * * Regardless of the particular label asserted by the State-whether it calls speech "commercial' or "commercial advertising' or "solicitation'-a court may not escape the task of assessing the First Amendment interest at stake and weighing it against the public interest allegedly served by the regulation. The diverse motives, means, and messages of advertising may make speech "commercial' in widely varying degrees. We need not decide here the extent to which constitutional protection is afforded commercial advertising under all circumstances and in the face of all kinds of regulation.

The task of balancing the interests at stake here was one that should have been undertaken by the Virginia courts before they reached their decision. We need not remand for that purpose, however, because the outcome is readily apparent from what has been said above.

In support of the statute, the appellee contends that the commercial operations of abortion referral agencies are associated with practices, such as fee splitting, that tend to diminish, or at least adversely affect, the quality of medical care, and that advertising of these operations will lead women to seek services from those who are interested only or mainly in financial gain apart from professional integrity and responsibility.

The State, of course, has a legitimate interest in maintaining the quality of medical care provided within its borders. No claim has been made, however, that this particular advertisement in any way affected the quality of medical services within Virginia. As applied to Bigelow's case, the statute was directed at the publishing of informative material relating to services offered in another State and was not directed at advertising by a referral agency or a practitioner whose activity Virginia had authority or power to regulate.

To be sure, the agency-advertiser's practices, although not then illegal, may later have proved to be at least "inimical to the public interest' in New York. (citation omitted) But this development would not justify a Virginia statute that forbids Virginians from using in New York the then legal services of a local New York agency. Here, Virginia is really asserting an interest in regulating what Virginians may hear or read about the New York services. It is, in effect, advancing an interest in shielding its citizens from information about activities outside Virginia's borders, activities that Virginia's police powers do not reach. This asserted interest, even if understandable, was entitled to little, if any, weight under the circumstances.

* * * *

We conclude that Virginia could not apply [the statute in question] to appellant's publication of the advertisement in question without unconstitutionally infringing upon his First Amendment rights. * * *

Decision

The judgment of Supreme Court of Virginia was reversed.

DE JONGE
v.
State of **OREGON**.
299 U.S. 353, 57 S.Ct. 255, 81 L.Ed. 278
Argued Dec. 9, 1936.
Decided Jan. 4, 1937.

Introduction

A freedom of assembly case involving a man convicted for holding a public meeting that was sponsored by the Communist Party. The Court overturned his conviction, ruling that the Oregon law restricted too much the rights of free speech and assembly. This case put the right of assembly on equal footing with the rights of free speech and press.

WESTLAW Summary

Dirk De Jonge was convicted of violating the Criminal Syndicalism Law of Oregon. The conviction was affirmed by the Supreme Court of Oregon, and Dirk De Jonge appeals.

Case Excerpts

Mr. Chief Justice HUGHES delivered the opinion of the Court.

Appellant, Dirk De Jonge, was indicted in Multnomah County, Oregon, for violation of the Criminal Syndicalism Law of that State. The act * * * defines "criminal syndicalism' as "the doctrine which advocates crime, physical violence, sabotage, or any unlawful acts or methods as a means of accomplishing or effecting industrial or political change or revolution.' With this preliminary definition the act proceeds to describe a number of offenses, embracing the teaching of criminal syndicalism, the printing or distribution of books, pamphlets, etc., advocating that doctrine, the organization of a society or assemblage which advocates it, and presiding at or assisting in conducting a meeting of such an organization, society or group. * * *

* * * The charge is that appellant assisted in the conduct of a meeting which was called under the auspices of the Communist Party, an organization advocating criminal syndicalism. The defense was that the meeting was public and orderly and was held for a lawful purpose; that, while it was held under the auspices of the Communist Party, neither criminal syndicalism nor any unlawful conduct was taught or advocated at the meeting either by appellant or by others. Appellant moved for a direction of acquittal, contending that the statute as applied to him, for merely assisting at a meeting called by the Communist Party at which nothing unlawful was done or advocated, violated the due process clause of the Fourteenth Amendment of the Constitution of the United States. This contention was overruled. Appellant was found guilty as charged and was sentenced to imprisonment for seven years. The judgment was affirmed by the Supreme Court of the State which considered the constitutional question and sustained the statute as thus applied. The case comes here on appeal.

* * * *

* * * The stipulation does not disclose any activity by the defendant as a basis for his prosecution other than his participation in the meeting in question. Nor does the stipulation show that the communist literature distributed at the meeting contained any advocacy of criminal syndicalism or of any unlawful conduct. It was admitted by the Attorney General of the State in his argument at the bar of this Court that the literature distributed in the meeting was not of that sort and that the extracts contained in the stipulation were taken from communist literature found elsewhere. Its introduction in evidence was for the purpose of showing that the Communist Party as such did advocate the doctrine of criminal syndicalism, a fact which is not disputed on this appeal.

* * * *

In this view, lack of sufficient evidence as to illegal advocacy or action at the meeting became immaterial. Having limited the charge to defendant's participation in a meeting called by the Communist Party, the state court sustained the conviction upon that basis regardless of what was said or done at the meeting.

We must take the indictment as thus construed. Conviction upon a charge not made would be sheer denial of due process. It thus appears that, while defendant was a member of the Communist Party, he was not indicted for participating in its organization, or for joining it, or for soliciting members or for distributing its literature. He was not charged with teaching or advocating criminal syndicalism or sabotage or any unlawful acts, either at the meeting or elsewhere. He was accordingly deprived of the benefit of evidence as to the orderly and lawful conduct of the meeting and that it was not called or used for the advocacy of criminal syndicalism or sabotage or any unlawful action. His sole offense as charged, and for which he was convicted and sentenced to imprisonment for seven years, was that he had assisted in the conduct of a public meeting, albeit otherwise lawful, which was held under the auspices of the Communist Party.

* * * *

We are not called upon to review the findings of the state court as to the objectives of the Communist Party. Notwithstanding those objectives, the defendant still enjoyed his personal right of free speech and to take part in a peaceable assembly having a lawful purpose, although called by that party. The defendant was none the less entitled to discuss the public issues of the day and thus in a lawful manner, without incitement to violence or crime, to seek redress of alleged grievances. That was of the essence of his guaranteed personal liberty.

We hold that the Oregon statute as applied to the particular charge as defined by the state court is repugnant to the due process clause of the Fourteenth Amendment. The judgment of conviction is reversed and the cause is remanded for further proceedings not inconsistent with this opinion.

Decision

Reversed, and cause remanded for further proceedings in accordance with opinion.

DENNIS et al.
v.
UNITED STATES.
341 U.S. 494, 71 S.Ct. 857, 95 L.Ed. 1137
Argued Dec. 4, 1950.
Decided June 4, 1951.

Introduction

A free speech and national security case in which the Court ruled that the Smith Act—a law against seditious speech—could be applied to members of the Communist Party. Eleven Communist Party leaders were convicted under that act and their convictions stood.

WESTLAW Summary

Eugene Dennis, and others, were convicted in the United States District Court for the Southern District of New York on an indictment for violation of Section 3 of the Smith Act, in that defendants conspired to organize the Communist Party of the United States as a group to teach and advocate the overthrow of the Government of the United States by force and violence and they appealed. To review a judgment of the Court of Appeals, L. Hand, Chief Judge, affirming the conviction, the defendants brought certiorari. The Supreme Court, Mr. Chief Justice Vinson, held that Section 2(a)(1), 2(a)(3), and 3 of the Smith Act do not inherently, or as construed or applied in the instant case, violate the First Amendment and other provisions of the Bill of Rights, and that they do not violate the First and Fifth Amendments because of indefiniteness.

Case Excerpts

Mr. Chief Justice VINSON announced the judgment of the Court.

* * * *

The indictment charged the petitioners with wilfully and knowingly conspiring (1) to organize as the Communist Party of the United States of America a society, group and assembly of persons who teach and advocate the overthrow and destruction of the Government of the United States by force and violence, and (2) knowingly and wilfully to advocate and teach the duty and necessity of overthrowing and destroying the Government of the United States by force and violence. * * *

The trial of the case extended over nine months, six of which were devoted to the taking of evidence, resulting in a record of 16,000 pages. Our limited grant of the writ of certiorari has removed from our consideration any question as to the sufficiency of the evidence to support the jury's determination that petitioners are guilty of the offense charged. Whether on this record petitioners did in fact advocate the overthrow of the Government by force and violence is not before us, and we must base any discussion of this point upon the conclusions stated in the opinion of the Court of Appeals, which treated the issue in great detail. That court held that the record in this case amply supports the necessary finding of the jury that petitioners, the leaders of the Communist Party in this country, were unwilling to work within our framework of democracy, but intended to initiate a violent revolution whenever the propitious occasion appeared. * * *

* * * *

The obvious purpose of the statute is to protect existing Government, not from change by peaceable, lawful and constitutional means, but from change by violence, revolution and terrorism. That it is within the power of the Congress to protect the Government of the United States from armed rebellion is a proposition which requires little discussion. * * * The question with which we are concerned here is not whether Congress has such power, but whether the means which it has employed conflict with the First and Fifth Amendments to the Constitution.

One of the bases for the contention that the means which Congress has employed are invalid takes the form of an attack on the face of the statute on the grounds that by its terms it prohibits academic discussion of the merits of Marxism-Leninism, that it stifles ideas and is contrary to all concepts of a free speech and a free press. Although we do not agree that the language itself has that significance, we must bear in mind that it is the duty of the federal courts to interpret federal legislation in a manner not inconsistent with the demands of the Constitution. * * *

The very language of the Smith Act negates the interpretation which petitioners would have us impose on that Act. It is directed at advocacy, not discussion. Thus, the trial judge properly charged the jury that they could not convict if they found that petitioners did "no more than pursue peaceful studies and discussions or teaching and advocacy in the realm of ideas.' He further charged that it was not unlawful "to conduct in an American college and university a course explaining the philosophical theories set forth in the books which have been placed in evidence.' Such a charge is in strict accord with the statutory language, and illustrates the meaning to be placed on those words. Congress did not intend to eradicate the free discussion of political theories, to destroy the traditional rights of Americans to discuss and evaluate ideas without fear of governmental sanction. Rather Congress was concerned with the very kind of activity in which the evidence showed these petitioners engaged.

* * * *

* * * Overthrow of the Government by force and violence is certainly a substantial enough interest for the Government to limit speech. Indeed, this is the ultimate value of any society, for if a society cannot protect its very structure from armed internal attack, it must follow that no subordinate value can be protected. If, then, this interest may be protected, the literal problem which is presented is what has been meant by the use of the phrase "clear and present danger' of the utterances bringing about the evil within the power of Congress to punish.

* * * *

Chief Judge Learned Hand, writing for the majority below, interpreted the phrase as follows: "In each case (courts) must ask whether the gravity of the "evil,' discounted by its improbability, justifies such invasion of free speech as is necessary to avoid the danger.' We adopt this statement of the rule. As articulated by Chief Judge Hand, it is as succinct and inclusive as any other we might devise at this time. It takes into consideration those factors which we deem relevant, and relates their significances. More we cannot expect from words.

Likewise, we are in accord with the court below, which affirmed the trial court's finding that the requisite danger existed. The mere fact that from the period 1945 to 1948 petitioners' activities did not result in an attempt to overthrow the Government by force and violence is of course no answer to the fact that there was a group that was ready to make the attempt. * * * If the ingredients of the reaction are present, we cannot bind the Government to wait until the catalyst is added.

* * * *

The question in this case is whether the statute which the legislature has enacted may be constitutionally applied. In other words, the Court must examine judicially the application of the statute to the particular situation, to ascertain if the Constitution prohibits the conviction. We hold that the statute may be applied where there is a "clear and present danger' of the substantive evil which the legislature had the right to prevent. Bearing, as it does, the marks of a "question of law,' the issue is properly one for the judge to decide.

* * * *

There remains to be discussed the question of vagueness-whether the statute as we have interpreted it is too vague, not sufficiently advising those who would speak of the limitations upon their activity. It is urged that such vagueness contravenes the First and Fifth Amendments.

* * *

We agree that the standard as defined is not a neat, mathematical formulary. Like all verbalizations it is subject to criticism on the score of indefiniteness. But petitioners themselves contend that the verbalization, "clear and present danger' is the proper standard. We see no difference, from the standpoint of vagueness, whether the standard of "clear and present danger' is one contained in haec verba within the statute, or whether it is the judicial measure of constitutional applicability. We have shown the indeterminate standard the phrase necessarily connotes. We do not think we have rendered that standard any more indefinite by our attempt to sum up the factors which are included within its scope. We think it well serves to indicate to those who would advocate constitutionally prohibited conduct that there is a line beyond which they may not go-a line which they, in full knowledge of what they intend and the circumstances in which their activity takes place, will well appreciate and understand. * * * Where there is doubt as to the intent of the defendants, the nature of their activities, or their power to bring about the evil, this Court will review the convictions with the scrupulous care demanded by our Constitution. But we are not convinced that because there may be borderline cases at some time in the future, these convictions should be reversed because of the argument that these petitioners could not know that their activities were constitutionally proscribed by the statute. * * *

We hold that ss 2(a)(1), 2(a)(3) and 3 of the Smith Act, do not inherently, or as construed or applied in the instant case, violate the First Amendment and other provisions of the Bill of Rights, or the First and Fifth Amendments because of indefiniteness. Petitioners intended to overthrow the Government of the United States as speedily as the circumstances would permit. Their conspiracy to organize the Communist Party and to teach and advocate the overthrow of the Government of the United States by force and violence created a "clear and present danger' of an attempt to overthrow the Government by force and violence. They were properly and constitutionally convicted for violation of the Smith Act. The judgments of conviction are affirmed.

Decision

Judgments affirmed.

DILLON
v.
GLOSS
256 U.S. 368, 41 S.Ct. 510, 65 L.Ed. 994
Argued March 22, 1921.
Decided May 16, 1921.

Introduction

A case ruling that allows Congress to place a "reasonable time limit" on the ratification process for amendments to the United States Constitution.

WESTLAW Summary

Appeal from the District Court of the United States for the Northern District of California.

Habeas corpus proceedings by J. J. Dillon against R. W. Gloss, Deputy Collector of Internal Revenue, to secure petitioner's discharge from custody under the National Prohibition Act. From an order denying the petition for the writ, petitioner appeals. Affirmed.

Case Excerpts

Mr. Justice VAN DEVANTER delivered the opinion of the Court.

This is an appeal from an order denying a petition for a writ of habeas corpus. The petitioner was in custody on a charge of transporting intoxicating liquor in violation of [the Eighteenth Amendment] and by his petition sought to be discharged on several grounds, all but two of which were abandoned after the decision in National Prohibition Cases, (citations omitted). The remaining grounds are, first, that the Eighteenth Amendment to the Constitution, is invalid, because the congressional resolution proposing the amendment declared that it should be inoperative unless ratified within seven years; and, secondly, that, in any event, the provisions of the act which the petitioner was charged with violating, and under which he was arrested, had not gone into effect at the time of the asserted violation nor at the time of the arrest.

The power to amend the Constitution and the mode of exerting it are dealt with in article 5, which reads:

"The Congress, whenever two thirds of both houses shall deem it necessary, shall propose amendments to this Constitution, or, on the application of the Legislatures of two thirds of the several states, shall call a convention for proposing amendments, which, in either case, shall be valid to all intents and purposes, as part of this Constitution, when ratified by the Legislatures of three fourths of the several states, or by conventions in three fourths thereof, as the one or the other mode of ratification may be proposed by the Congress: Provided that no amendment which may be made prior to the year one thousand eight hundred and eight shall in any manner affect the first and fourth clauses in the ninth section of the first article; and that no state, without its consent, shall be deprived of its equal suffrage in the Senate.'

It will be seen that this article says nothing about the time within which ratification may be had-neither that it shall be unlimited nor that it shall be fixed by Congress. What then is the reasonable inference or implication? Is it that ratification may be had at any time, as within a few years, a century or even a longer period, or that it must be had within some reasonable period which Congress is left free to define? Neither the debates in the federal convention which framed the Constitution nor those in the state conventions which ratified it shed any light on the question.

The proposal for the Eighteenth Amendment is the first in which a definite period for ratification was fixed. Theretofore 21 amendments had been proposed by Congress and seventeen of these had been ratified by the Legislatures of three fourths of the states-some within a single year after their proposal and all within four years. Each of the remaining 4 had been ratified in some of the states, but not in a sufficient number. Eighty years after the partial ratification of one, an effort was made to complete its ratification, and the Legislature of Ohio passed a joint resolution to that end, after which the effort was abandoned. Two, after ratification in one less than the required number of states had lain dormant for a century. The other, proposed March 2, 1861, declared:

"No amendment shall be made to the Constitution which will authorize or give to Congress the power to abolish or interfere, within any state, with the domestic institutions thereof, including that of persons held to labor or service by the laws of said state.'

Its principal purpose was to protect slavery and at the time of its proposal and partial ratification it was a subject of absorbing interest, but after the adoption of the Thirteenth Amendment it was generally forgotten. Whether an amendment proposed without fixing any time for ratification, and which after favorable action in less than the required number of states had lain dormant for many years, could be resurrected and its ratification completed had been mooted on several occasions, but was still an open question.

These were the circumstances in the light of which Congress in proposing the Eighteenth Amendment fixed seven years as the period for ratification. Whether this could be done was questioned at the time and debated at length, but the prevailing view in both houses was that some limitation was intended and that seven years was a reasonable period.

(1) That the Constitution contains no express provision on the subject is not in itself controlling; for with the Constitution, as with a statute or other written instrument, what is reasonably implied is as much a part of it as what is expressed. * * * When proposed in either mode amendments to be effective must be ratified by the Legislatures, or by conventions, in three-fourths of the states, "as the one or the other mode of ratification may be proposed by the Congress.' Thus the people of the United States, by whom the Constitution was ordained and established, have made it a condition to amending that instrument that the amendment be submitted to representative assemblies in the several states and be ratified in three-fourths of them. The plain meaning of this is (a) that all amendments must have the sanction of the people of the United States, the original fountain of power, acting through representative assemblies, and (b) that ratification by these assemblies in three-fourths of the states shall be taken as a decisive expression of the people's will and be binding on all.

(2) We do not find anything in the article which suggests that an amendment once proposed is to be open to ratification for all time, or that ratification in some of the states may be separated from that in others by many years and yet be effective. We do find that which strongly suggests the contrary. First, proposal and ratification are not treated as unrelated acts, but as succeeding steps in a single endeavor, the natural

inference being that they are not to be widely separated in time. Secondly, it is only when there is deemed to be a necessity therefor that amendments are to be proposed, the reasonable implication being that when proposed they are to be considered and disposed of presently. Thirdly, as ratification is but the expression of the approbation of the people and is to be effective when had in three-fourths of the states, there is a fair implication that it must be sufficiently contemporaneous in that number of states to reflect the will of the people in all sections at relatively the same period, which of course ratification scattered through a long series of years would not do. * * * We conclude * * * that the ratification must be within some reasonable time after the proposal.

(3, 4) Of the power of Congress, keeping within reasonable limits, to fix a definite period for the ratification we entertain no doubt. * * * * Whether a definite period for ratification shall be fixed, so that all may know what it is and speculation on what is a reasonable time may be avoided, is, in our opinion, a matter of detail which Congress may determine as an incident of its power to designate the mode of ratification. It is not questioned that seven years, the period fixed in this instance, was reasonable, if power existed to fix a definite time; nor could it well be questioned considering the periods within which prior amendments were ratified.

(5, 6) The provisions of the act which the petitioner was charged with violating and under which he was arrested were by the terms of the act to be in force from and after the date when the Eighteenth Amendment should go into effect, and the latter by its own terms was to go into effect one year after being ratified. Its ratification, of which we take judicial notice, was consummated January 16, 1919. That the Secretary of State did not proclaim its ratification until January 29, 1919, is not material, for the date of its consummation, and not that on which it is proclaimed, controls. It follows that the provisions of the act with which the petitioner is concerned went into effect January 16, 1920. His alleged offense and his arrest were on the following day; so his claim that those provisions had not gone into effect at the time is not well grounded.

Decision

Final order affirmed.

Danny **ESCOBEDO**
v.
State of **ILLINOIS.**
378 U.S. 478, 84 S.Ct. 1758, 12 L.Ed.2d 977.
Argued April 29, 1964.
Decided June 22, 1964.

Introduction

A rights of the accused/right to counsel case in which the Supreme Court overturned the conviction of Danny Escobedo who had been arrested by Chicago police in connection with the murder of his brother-in-law. Escobedo's request to see his lawyer had been refused even though the lawyer was in the police station trying to see him during his questioning.

WESTLAW Summary

The defendant was convicted in the Criminal Court, Cook County, Illinois, of murder, and he brought error. The Supreme Court of Illinois affirmed. Certiorari was granted. The Supreme Court held that where the investigation is no longer a general inquiry into unsolved crime but has begun to focus upon a particular suspect, the suspect has been taken into police custody, the police carry out a process of interrogations that lends itself to eliciting incriminating statements, the suspect has requested and been denied opportunity to consult with his lawyer, and police have not effectively warned him of his absolute constitutional right to remain silent, the accused has been denied assistance of counsel in violation of Sixth Amendment as made obligatory upon the states by Fourteenth Amendment, and no statement elicited by police during interrogation may be used against him at criminal trial.

Case Excerpts

Mr. Justice GOLDBERG delivered the opinion of the Court.

The critical question in this case is whether, under the circumstances, the refusal by the police to honor petitioner's request to consult with his lawyer during the course of an interrogation constitutes a denial of "the Assistance of Counsel' in violation of the Sixth Amendment to the Constitution as "made obligatory upon the States by the Fourteenth Amendment,' (citation omitted) and thereby renders inadmissible in a state criminal trial any incriminating statement elicited by the police during the interrogation.

On the night of January 19, 1960, petitioner's brother-in-law was fatally shot. In the early hours of the next morning, at 2:30 a.m., petitioner was arrested without a warrant and interrogated. Petitioner made no statement to the police and was released at 5 that afternoon pursuant to a state court writ of habeas corpus obtained by Mr. Warren Wolfson, a lawyer who had been retained by petitioner.

On January 30, Benedict DiGerlando, who was then in police custody and who was later indicted for the murder along with petitioner, told the police that petitioner had fired the fatal shots. Between 8 and 9 that evening, petitioner and his sister, the widow of the deceased, were arrested and taken to police headquarters. En route to the police station, the police "had handcuffed the defendant behind his back,' and "one of the arresting officers told defendant that DiGerlando had named him as the one who shot' the deceased. Petitioner testified, without contradiction, that the "detective said they had us pretty well, up pretty tight, and we might as well admit to this crime,' and that he replied, "I am sorry but I would like to have advice from my lawyer.' A police officer testified that although petitioner was not formally charged "he was in custody' and "couldn't walk out the door.'

* * * *

Petitioner testified that during the course of the interrogation he repeatedly asked to speak to his lawyer and that the police said that his lawyer "didn't want to see' him. The testimony of the police officers confirmed these accounts in substantial detail.

Notwithstanding repeated requests by each, petitioner and his retained lawyer were afforded no opportunity to consult during the course of the entire interrogation. At one point, as previously noted, petitioner and his attorney came into each other's view for a few moments but the attorney was quickly ushered away. Petitioner testified "that he heard a detective telling the attorney the latter would not be allowed to talk to (him) "until they were done" and that he heard the attorney being refused permission to remain in the adjoining room. A police officer testified that he had told the lawyer that he could not see petitioner until "we were through interrogating' him.

* * * *

A police officer testified that during the interrogation the following occurred: "I informed him of what DiGerlando told me and when I did, he told me that DiGerlando was (lying) and I said, "Would you care to tell DiGerlando that?' and he said, "Yes, I will.' So, I brought * * * Escobedo in and he confronted DiGerlando and he told him that he was lying and said, "I didn't shoot Manuel, you did it."

In this way, petitioner, for the first time admitted to some knowledge of the crime. After that he made additional statements further implicating himself in the murder plot. At this point an Assistant State's Attorney, Theodore J. Cooper, was summoned "to take' a statement. Mr. Cooper, an experienced lawyer who was assigned to the Homicide Division to take "statements from some defendants and some prisoners that they had in custody,' "took' petitioner's statement by asking carefully framed questions apparently designed to assure the admissibility into evidence of the resulting answers. Mr. Cooper testified that he did not advise petitioner of his constitutional rights, and it is undisputed that no one during the course of the interrogation so advised him.

Petitioner moved both before and during trial to suppress the incriminating statement, but the motions were denied. Petitioner was convicted of murder and he appealed the conviction.

The Supreme Court of Illinois, in its original opinion of February 1, 1963, held the statement inadmissible and reversed the conviction. The court said:

"(I)t seems manifest to us, from the undisputed evidence and the circumstances surrounding defendant at the time of his statement and shortly prior thereto, that the defendant understood he would be permitted to go home if he gave the statement and would be granted an immunity from prosecution.'

* * * *

The interrogation here was conducted before petitioner was formally indicted. But in the context of this case, that fact should make no difference. When petitioner requested, and was denied, an opportunity to consult with his lawyer, the investigation had ceased to be a general investigation of "an unsolved crime.' (citation omitted). Petitioner had become the accused, and the purpose of the interrogation was to "get him' to confess his guilt despite his constitutional right not to do so. At the time of his arrest and throughout the course of the interrogation, the police told petitioner that they had convincing evidence that he had fired the fatal shots. Without informing him of his absolute right to remain silent in the face of this accusation, the police urged him to make a statement. * * *

* * * *

It is argued that if the right to counsel is afforded prior to indictment, the number of confessions obtained by the police will diminish significantly, because most confessions are obtained during the period between arrest and indictment * * *. This argument, of course, cuts two ways. The fact that many confessions are obtained during this period points up its critical nature as a "stage when legal aid and advice' are surely needed. (citations omitted). The right to counsel would indeed be hollow if it began at a period when few confessions were obtained. There is necessarily a direct relationship between the importance of a stage to the police in their quest for a confession and the criticalness of that stage to the accused in his need for legal advice. Our Constitution, unlike some others, strikes the balance in favor of the right of the accused to be advised by his lawyer of his privilege against self-incrimination. * * *

* * * *

We have also learned the companion lesson of history that no system of criminal justice can, or should, survive if it comes to depend for its continued effectiveness on the citizens' abdication through unawareness of their constitutional rights. No system worth preserving should have to fear that if an accused is permitted to consult with a lawyer, he will become aware of, and exercise, these rights. If the exercise of constitutional rights will thwart the effectiveness of a system of law enforcement, then there is something very wrong with that system.

* * * *

The judgment of the Illinois Supreme Court is reversed and the case remanded for proceedings not inconsistent with this opinion.

Decision

Reversed and remanded.

EVERSON
v.
BOARD OF EDUCATION of Ewing TP. et al.
330 U.S. 1, 67 S.Ct. 504, 91 L.Ed. 711
Argued Nov. 20, 1946.
Decided Feb. 10, 1947.
Rehearing Denied March 10, 1947.

Introduction

A First Amendment/establishment clause case in which the Court ruled in favor of tax-supported busing of students who attended parochial schools.

WESTLAW Summary

Certiorari proceedings by Arch R. Everson to set aside a resolution of the Board of Education of the Township of Ewing, in the County of Mercer, state of New Jersey, providing for the transportation of pupils to both public and parochial schools. A judgment setting aside the resolution was reversed by the Court of Errors and Appeals of New Jersey, and petitioner appeals.

Case Excerpts

Mr. Justice BLACK delivered the opinion of the Court.

A New Jersey statute authorizes its local school districts to make rules and contracts for the transportation of children to and from schools. The appellee, a township board of education, acting pursuant to this statute authorized reimbursement to parents of money expended by them for the bus transportation of their children on regular busses operated by the public transportation system. Part of this money was for the payment of transportation of some children in the community to Catholic parochial schools. These church schools give their students, in addition to secular education, regular religious instruction conforming to the religious tenets and modes of worship of the Catholic Faith. The superintendent of these schools is a Catholic priest.

The appellant, in his capacity as a district taxpayer, filed suit in a State court challenging the right of the Board to reimburse parents of parochial school students. He contended that the statute and the resolution passed pursuant to it violated both the State and the Federal Constitutions. That court held that the legislature was without power to authorize such payment under the State constitution. The New Jersey Court of Errors and Appeals reversed, holding that neither the statute nor the resolution passed pursuant to it was in conflict with the State constitution or the provisions of the Federal Constitution in issue. The case is here on appeal * * *.

* * * *

The only contention here is that the State statute and the resolution, in so far as they authorized reimbursement to parents of children attending parochial schools, violate the Federal Constitution in these two respects, which to some extent, overlap. First. They authorize the State to take by taxation the private property of some and bestow it upon others, to be used for their own private purposes. This, it is alleged violates the due process clause of the Fourteenth Amendment. Second. The statute and the resolution forced inhabitants to pay taxes to help support and maintain schools which are dedicated to, and which regularly teach, the Catholic Faith. This is alleged to be a use of State power to support church schools contrary to the prohibition of the First Amendment which the Fourteenth Amendment made applicable to the states.

First. The due process argument that the State law taxes some people to help others carry out their private purposes is framed in two phases. The first phase is that a state cannot tax A to reimburse B for the cost of transporting his children to church schools. This is said to violate the due process clause because the children are sent to these church schools to satisfy the personal desires of their parents, rather than the public's interest in the general education of all children. This argument, if valid, would apply equally to prohibit state payment for the transportation of children to any non-public school, whether operated by a church, or any other nongovernment individual or group. But, the New Jersey legislature has decided that a public purpose will be served by using tax-raised funds to pay the bus fares of all school children, including those who attend parochial schools. The New Jersey Court of Errors and Appeals has reached the same conclusion. The fact that a state law, passed to satisfy a public need, coincides with the personal desires of the individuals most directly affected is certainly an inadequate reason for us to say that a legislature has erroneously appraised the public need.

* * * *

Insofar as the second phase of the due process argument may differ from the first, it is by suggesting that taxation for transportation of children to church schools constitutes support of a religion by the State. But if the law is invalid for this reason, it is because it violates the First Amendment's prohibition against the establishment of religion by law. This is the exact question raised by appellant's second contention, to consideration of which we now turn.

Second. The New Jersey statute is challenged as a "law respecting an establishment of religion.' The First Amendment, as made applicable to the states by the Fourteenth, commands that a state "shall make no law respecting an establishment of religion, or prohibiting the free exercise thereof.' These words of the First Amendment reflected in the minds of early Americans a vivid mental picture of conditions and practices which they fervently wished to stamp out in order to preserve liberty for themselves and for their posterity. Doubtless their goal has not been entirely reached; but so far has the Nation moved toward it that the expression "law respecting an establishment of religion,' probably does not so vividly remind present-day Americans of the evils, fears, and political problems that caused that expression to be written into our Bill of Rights. Whether this New Jersey law is one respecting the "establishment of religion' requires an understanding of the meaning of that language, particularly with respect to the imposition of taxes. Once again, therefore, it is not inappropriate briefly to review the background and environment of the period in which that constitutional language was fashioned and adopted.

* * * *

The "establishment of religion' clause of the First Amendment means at least this: Neither a state nor the Federal Government can set up a church. Neither can pass laws which aid one religion, aid all religions, or prefer one religion over another. Neither can force nor influence a person to go to or to remain away from church against his will or force him to profess a belief or disbelief in any religion. No person can be punished for entertaining or professing religious beliefs or disbeliefs, for church attendance or non-attendance. No tax in any amount, large or small, can be levied to support any religious activities or institutions, whatever they may be called, or whatever from they may adopt to teach or practice religion. Neither a state nor the Federal Government can, openly or secretly, participate in the affairs of any religious organizations or groups and vice versa. * * *

We must consider the New Jersey statute in accordance with the foregoing limitations imposed by the First Amendment. But we must not strike that state statute down if it is within the state's constitutional power even though it approaches the verge of that power. New Jersey cannot consistently with the "establishment of religion' clause of the First Amendment contribute tax-raised funds to the support of an institution which teaches the tenets and faith of any church. On the other hand, other language of the amendment commands that New Jersey cannot hamper its citizens in the free exercise of their own religion. Consequently, it cannot exclude individual Catholics, Lutherans, Mohammedans, Baptists, Jews, Methodists, Non-believers, Presbyterians, or the members of any other faith, because of their faith, or lack of it, from receiving the benefits of public welfare legislation. While we do not mean to intimate that a state could not provide transportation only to children attending public schools, we must be careful, in protecting the citizens of New Jersey against state-established churches, to be sure that we do not inadvertently prohibit New Jersey from extending its general State law benefits to all its citizens without regard to their religious belief.

Measured by these standards, we cannot say that the First Amendment prohibits New Jersey from spending tax-raised funds to pay the bus fares of parochial school pupils as a part of a general program under which it pays the fares of pupils attending public and other schools. It is undoubtedly true that children are helped to get to church schools. There is even a possibility that some of the children might not be sent to the church schools if the parents were compelled to pay their children's bus fares out of their own pockets when transportation to a public school would have been paid for by the State. * * *

This Court has said that parents may, in the discharge of their duty under state compulsory education laws, send their children to a religious rather than a public school if the school meets the secular educational requirements which the state has power to impose. It appears that these parochial schools meet New Jersey's requirements. The State contributes no money to the schools. It does not support them. Its legislation, as applied, does no more than provide a general program to help parents get their children, regardless of their religion, safely and expeditiously to and from accredited schools.

The First Amendment has erected a wall between church and state. That wall must be kept high and impregnable. We could not approve the slightest breach. New Jersey has not breached it here.

Decision

Affirmed.

Alvin Bernard **FORD**, etc.
v.
Louie L. **WAINWRIGHT**
477 U.S. 399, 106 S.Ct. 2595, 91 L.Ed.2d 335
Argued April 22, 1986.
Decided June 26, 1986.

Introduction

An Eighth Amendment/capital punishment case in which the Court ruled that the U.S. Constitution bars states from executing convicted killers who have become insane while waiting on death row.

WESTLAW Summary

A habeas corpus petition was filed on behalf of a death row prisoner. The United States District Court for the Southern District of Florida denied the petition, and appeal was taken. The United States Court of Appeals for the Eleventh Circuit, affirmed and denied rehearing, and the petitioner sought review. The Supreme Court, Justice Marshall held that: (1) Eighth Amendment prohibits state from inflicting the penalty of death upon a prisoner who is insane, and (2) Florida's procedures for determining sanity of a death row prisoner was not "adequate to afford a full and fair hearing" on the critical issue and therefore the habeas petitioner was entitled to an evidentiary hearing in the district court, de novo, on the question of his competence to be executed.

Case Excerpts

Justice MARSHALL announced the judgment of the Court.

For centuries no jurisdiction has countenanced the execution of the insane, yet this Court has never decided whether the Constitution forbids the practice. Today we keep faith with our common-law heritage in holding that it does.

Alvin Bernard Ford was convicted of murder in 1974 and sentenced to death. There is no suggestion that he was incompetent at the time of his offense, at trial, or at sentencing. In early 1982, however, Ford began to manifest gradual changes in behavior. They began as an occasional peculiar idea or confused perception, but became more serious over time. After reading in the newspaper that the Ku Klux Klan had held a rally in nearby Jacksonville, Florida, Ford developed an obsession focused upon the Klan. His letters to various people reveal endless brooding about his "Klan work," and an increasingly pervasive delusion that he had become the target of a complex conspiracy, involving the Klan and assorted others, designed to force him to commit suicide. He believed that the prison guards, part of the conspiracy, had been killing people and putting the bodies in the concrete enclosures used for beds. Later, he began to believe that his women relatives were being tortured and sexually abused somewhere in the prison. This notion developed into a delusion that the people who were tormenting him at the prison had taken members of Ford's family hostage. The hostage delusion took firm hold and expanded, until Ford was reporting that 135 of his friends and family were being held hostage in the prison, and that only he could help them. By "day 287" of the "hostage crisis," the list of hostages had expanded to include "senators, Senator Kennedy, and many other leaders." In a letter to the Attorney General of Florida, written in 1983, Ford appeared to assume authority for ending the "crisis," claiming to have fired a number of prison officials. He began to refer to himself as "Pope John Paul, III," and reported having appointed nine new justices to the Florida Supreme Court.

* * * *

Since this Court last had occasion to consider the infliction of the death penalty upon the insane, our interpretations of the Due Process Clause and the Eighth Amendment have evolved substantially. * * * Now that the Eighth Amendment has been recognized to affect significantly both the procedural and the substantive aspects of the death penalty, the question of executing the insane takes on a wholly different complexion. The adequacy of the procedures chosen by a State to determine sanity, therefore, will depend upon an issue that this Court has never addressed: whether the Constitution places a substantive restriction on the State's power to take the life of an insane prisoner.

* * * *

The Eighth Amendment prohibits the State from inflicting the penalty of death upon a prisoner who is insane. Petitioner's allegation of insanity in his habeas corpus petition, if proved, therefore, would bar his execution. The question before us is whether the District Court was under an obligation to hold an evidentiary hearing on the question of Ford's sanity. In answering that question, we bear in mind that, while the underlying social values encompassed by the Eighth Amendment are rooted in historical traditions, the manner in which our judicial system protects those values is purely a matter of contemporary law. Once a substantive right or restriction is recognized in the Constitution, therefore, its enforcement is in no way confined to the rudimentary process deemed adequate in ages past.

* * * *

Florida law directs the Governor, when informed that a person under sentence of death may be insane, to stay the execution and appoint a commission of three psychiatrists to examine the prisoner. * * * After receiving the report of the commission, the Governor must determine whether "the convicted person has the mental capacity to understand the nature of the death penalty and the reasons why it was imposed on him." If the Governor finds that the prisoner has that capacity, then a death warrant is issued; if not, then the prisoner is committed to a mental health facility. The procedure is conducted wholly within the executive branch, ex parte, and provides the exclusive means for determining sanity. Ford v. Wainwright,

Petitioner received the statutory process. The Governor selected three psychiatrists, who together interviewed Ford for a total of 30 minutes, in the presence of eight other people, including Ford's counsel, the State's attorneys, and correctional officials. * * * That this most cursory form of procedural review fails to achieve even the minimal degree of reliability required for the protection of any constitutional interest * * * is self-evident.

The first deficiency in Florida's procedure lies in its failure to include the prisoner in the truth-seeking process. * * * [S]tate practice does not permit any material relevant to the ultimate decision to be submitted on behalf of the prisoner facing execution. In all other proceedings leading to the execution of an accused, we have said that the factfinder must "have before it all possible relevant information about the individual defendant whose fate it must determine." * * * It would be odd were we now to abandon our insistence upon unfettered presentation of relevant information, before the final fact antecedent to execution has been found.

Rather, consistent with the heightened concern for fairness and accuracy that has characterized our review of the process requisite to the taking of a human life, we believe that any procedure that precludes the prisoner or his counsel from presenting material relevant to his sanity or bars consideration of that material by the factfinder is necessarily inadequate. * * *

A related flaw in the Florida procedure is the denial of any opportunity to challenge or impeach the state-appointed psychiatrists' opinions. * * * Cross-examination of the psychiatrists, or perhaps a less formal equivalent, would contribute markedly to the process of seeking truth in sanity disputes by bringing to light the bases for each expert's beliefs, the precise factors underlying those beliefs, any history of error or caprice of the examiner, any personal bias with respect to the issue of capital punishment, the expert's degree of certainty about his or her own conclusions, and the precise meaning of ambiguous words used in the report. Without some questioning of the experts concerning their technical conclusions, a factfinder simply cannot be expected to evaluate the various opinions, particularly when they are themselves inconsistent. * * * The failure of the Florida procedure to afford the prisoner's representative any opportunity to clarify or challenge the state experts' opinions or methods creates a significant possibility that the ultimate decision made in reliance on those experts will be distorted.

Perhaps the most striking defect * * * is the State's placement of the decision wholly within the executive branch. Under this procedure, the person who appoints the experts and ultimately decides whether the State will be able to carry out the sentence that it has long sought is the Governor, whose subordinates have been responsible for initiating every stage of the prosecution of the condemned from arrest through sentencing. The commander of the State's corps of prosecutors cannot be said to have the neutrality that is necessary for reliability in the factfinding proceeding. * * *

Having identified various failings of the Florida scheme, we must conclude that the State's procedures for determining sanity are inadequate to preclude federal redetermination of the constitutional issue. We do not here suggest that only a full trial on the issue of sanity will suffice to protect the federal interests; we leave to the State the task of developing appropriate ways to enforce the constitutional restriction upon its execution of sentences. It may be that some high threshold showing on behalf of the prisoner will be found a necessary means to control the number of nonmeritorious or repetitive claims of insanity. * * *

* * * *

The judgment of the Court of Appeals is reversed, and the case remanded for further proceedings consistent with this opinion.

Decision

Reversed and remanded.

Clarence Earl **GIDEON**
v.
Louie L. **WAINWRIGHT**
372 U.S. 335, 83 S.Ct. 792, 9 L.Ed.2d 799
Argued Jan. 15, 1963.
Decided March 18, 1963.

Introduction

A rights of the accused/right to counsel in which the Court said that persons who can demonstrate that they are unable to afford to have lawyer present and are accused of felonies must be given a lawyer at the expense of the government.

WESTLAW Summary

The petitioner brought habeas corpus proceedings against the Director of the Division of Corrections. The Florida Supreme Court denied all relief, and the petitioner brought certiorari. The United States Supreme Court, held that the Sixth Amendment to the federal Constitution providing that in all criminal prosecutions the accused shall enjoy right to assistance of counsel for his defense is made obligatory on the states by the Fourteenth Amendment, and that an indigent defendant in a criminal prosecution in a state court has the right to have counsel appointed for him.

Case Excerpts

Mr. Justice BLACK delivered the opinion of the Court.

Petitioner was charged in a Florida state court with having broken and entered a poolroom with intent to commit a misdemeanor. This offense is a felony under Florida law. Appearing in court without funds and without a lawyer, petitioner asked the court to appoint counsel for him, whereupon the following colloquy took place:

"The COURT: Mr. Gideon, I am sorry, but I cannot appoint Counsel to represent you in this case. Under the laws of the State of

Florida, the only time the Court can appoint Counsel to represent a Defendant is when that person is charged with a capital offense. I am sorry, but I will have to deny your request to appoint Counsel to defend you in this case.

"The DEFENDANT: The United States Supreme Court says I am entitled to be represented by Counsel.'

Put to trial before a jury, Gideon conducted his defense about as well as could be expected from a layman. He made an opening statement to the jury, cross-examined the State's witnesses, presented witnesses in his own defense, declined to testify himself, and made a short argument "emphasizing his innocence to the charge contained in the Information filed in this case.' The jury returned a verdict of guilty, and petitioner was sentenced to serve five years in the state prison. Later, petitioner filed in the Florida Supreme Court this habeas corpus petitioner attacking his conviction and sentence on the ground that the trial court's refusal to appoint counsel for him denied him rights "guaranteed by the Constitution and the Bill of Rights by the United States Government.' Treating the petition for habeas corpus as properly before it, the State Supreme Court, "upon consideration thereof' but without an opinion, denied all relief. Since 1942, when Betts v. Brady (citation omitted) was decided by a divided Court, the problem of a defendant's federal constitutional right to counsel in a state court has been a continuing source of controversy and litigation in both state and federal courts To give this problem another review here, we granted certiorari. Since Gideon was proceeding in forma pauperis, we appointed counsel to represent him and requested both sides to discuss in their briefs and oral arguments the following: "Should this Court's holding in Betts v. Brady, be reconsidered?'

The facts upon which Betts claimed that he had been unconstitutionally denied the right to have counsel appointed to assist him are strikingly like the facts upon which Gideon here bases his federal constitutional claim. Betts was indicted for robbery in a Maryland state court. On arraignment, he told the trial judge of his lack of funds to hire a lawyer and asked the court to appoint one for him. Betts was advised that it was not the practice in that county to appoint counsel for indigent defendants except in murder and rape cases. He then pleaded not guilty, had witnesses summoned, cross-examined the State's witnesses, examined his own, and chose not to testify himself. He was found guilty by the judge, sitting without a jury, and sentenced to eight years in prison. Like Gideon, Betts sought release by habeas corpus, alleging that he had been denied the right to assistance of counsel in violation of the Fourteenth Amendment. Betts was denied any relief, and on review this Court affirmed. It was held that a refusal to appoint counsel for an indigent defendant charged with a felony did not necessarily violate the Due Process Clause of the Fourteenth Amendment, which for reasons given the Court deemed to be the only applicable federal constitutional provision. * * * Since the facts and circumstances of the two cases are so nearly indistinguishable, we think the Betts v. Brady holding if left standing would require us to reject Gideon's claim that the Constitution guarantees him the assistance of counsel. Upon full reconsideration we conclude that Betts v. Brady should be overruled.

The Sixth Amendment provides, "In all criminal prosecutions, the accused shall enjoy the right * * * to have the Assistance of Counsel for his defence.' We have construed this to mean that in federal courts counsel must be provided for defendants unable to employ counsel unless the right is competently and intelligently waived. Betts argued that this right is extended to indigent defendants in state courts by the Fourteenth Amendment. In response the Court stated that, while the Sixth Amendment laid down "no rule for the conduct of the states, the question recurs whether the constraint laid by the amendment upon the national courts expresses a rule so fundamental and essential to a fair trial, and so, to due process of law, that it is made obligatory upon the states by the Fourteenth Amendment.' In order to decide whether the Sixth Amendment's guarantee of counsel is of this fundamental nature, the Court in Betts set out and considered "(r)elevant data on the subject * * * afforded by constitutional and statutory provisions subsisting in the colonies and the states prior to the inclusion of the Bill of Rights in the national Constitution, and in the constitutional, legislative, and judicial history of the states to the present date.' On the basis of this historical data the Court concluded that "appointment of counsel is not a fundamental right, essential to a fair trial.' * * *

* * * *

We accept Betts v. Brady's assumption, based as it was on our prior cases, that a provision of the Bill of Rights which is "fundamental and essential to a fair trial' is made obligatory upon the States by the

Fourteenth Amendment. We think the Court in Betts was wrong, however, in concluding that the Sixth Amendment's guarantee of counsel is not one of these fundamental rights. * * *

* * * *

The fact is that in deciding as it did-that "appointment of counsel is not a fundamental right, essential to a fair trial'-the Court in Betts v. Brady made an abrupt break with its own well-considered precedents. In returning to these old precedents, sounder we believe than the new, we but restore constitutional principles established to achieve a fair system of justice. Not only these precedents but also reason and reflection require us to recognize that in our adversary system of criminal justice, any person haled into court, who is too poor to hire a lawyer, cannot be assured a fair trial unless counsel is provided for him. This seems to us to be an obvious truth. Governments, both state and federal, quite properly spend vast sums of money to establish machinery to try defendants accused of crime. Lawyers to prosecute are everywhere deemed essential to protect the public's interest in an orderly society. Similarly, there are few defendants charged with crime, few indeed, who fail to hire the best lawyers they can get to prepare and present their defenses. That government hires lawyers to prosecute and defendants who have the money hire lawyers to defend are the strongest indications of the wide-spread belief that lawyers in criminal courts are necessities, not luxuries. The right of one charged with crime to counsel may not be deemed fundamental and essential to fair trials in some countries, but it is in ours. From the very beginning, our state and national constitutions and laws have laid great emphasis on procedural and substantive safeguards designed to assure fair trials before impartial tribunals in which every defendant stands equal before the law. This noble ideal cannot be realized if the poor man charged with crime has to face his accusers without a lawyer to assist him. * * *

The Court in Betts v. Brady departed from the sound wisdom upon which the Court's holding in Powell v. Alabama rested. Florida, supported by two other States, has asked that Betts v. Brady be left intact. Twenty-two States, as friends of the Court, argue that Betts was "an anachronism when handed down' and that it should now be overruled. We agree.

The judgment is reversed and the cause is remanded to the Supreme Court of Florida for further action not inconsistent with this opinion.

Decision

Reversed.

GITLOW
v.
People of the State of **NEW YORK.**
268 U.S. 652, 45 S.Ct. 625, 69 L.Ed. 1138
Reargued Nov. 23, 1923.
Decided June 8, 1925.

Introduction

A free speech/bad-tendency rule case which allows First Amendment freedoms to be curtailed if there is a possibility that such expression might lead to some evil. In this case, a member of a left-wing group was convicted of violating New York State's criminal anarchy statute when he published and distributed materials urging the violent overthrow of the United States government.

WESTLAW Summary

Benjamin Gitlow was convicted of statutory crime of criminal anarchy. To review a judgment of the Court of Appeals of New York, affirming a judgment of the Appellate Division, he brings error. Judgment affirmed.

Case Excerpts

Mr. Justice SANFORD delivered the opinion of the Court.

Benjamin Gitlow was indicted in the Supreme Court of New York, with three others, for the statutory crime of criminal anarchy. He was separately tried, convicted, and sentenced to imprisonment. The judgment was affirmed by the Appellate Division and by the Court of Appeals. The case is here on writ of error to the Supreme Court, to which the record was remitted.

The contention here is that the statute, by its terms and as applied in this case, is repugnant to the due process clause of the Fourteenth Amendment. * * *

* * * *

The following facts were established on the trial by undisputed evidence and admissions: The defendant is a member of the Left Wing Section of the Socialist Party, a dissenting branch or faction of that party formed in opposition to its dominant policy of "moderate Socialism.' Membership in both is open to aliens as well as citizens. The Left Wing Section was organized nationally at a conference in New York City in June, 1919, attended by ninety delegates from twenty different States. The conference elected a National Council, of which the defendant was a member, and left to it the adoption of a "Manifesto.' This was published in The Revolutionary Age, the official organ of the Left Wing. The defendant was on the board of managers of the paper and was its business manager. He arranged for the printing of the paper and took to the printer the manuscript of the first issue which contained the Left Wing Manifesto, and also a Communist Program and a Program of the Left Wing that had been adopted by the conference. Sixteen thousand copies were printed, which were delivered at the premises in New York City used as the office of the Revolutionary Age and the head quarters of the Left Wing, and occupied by the defendant and other officials. These copies were paid for by the defendant, as business manager of the paper. Employees at this office wrapped and mailed out copies of the paper under the defendant's direction; and copies were sold from this office. It was admitted that the defendant signed a card subscribing to the Manifesto and Program of the Left Wing, which all applicants were required to sign before being admitted to membership; that he went to different parts of the State to speak to branches of the Socialist Party about the principles of the Left Wing and advocated their adoption; and that he was responsible for the Manifesto as it appeared, that "he knew of the publication, in a general way and he knew of its publication afterwards, and is responsible for the circulation.'

There was no evidence of any effect resulting from the publication and circulation of the Manifesto.

No witnesses were offered in behalf of the defendant.

* * * *

The Court of Appeals held that the Manifesto "advocated the overthrow of this government by violence, or by unlawful means.' In one of the opinions representing the views of a majority of the court, it was said:

"It will be seen * * * that this defendant through the Manifesto * * * advocated the destruction of the state and the establishment of the dictatorship of the proletariat. * * * To advocate * * * the commission of this conspiracy or action by mass strike whereby government is cripped, the administration of justice paralyzed, and the health, morals and welfare of a community endangered, and this for the purpose of bringing about a revolution in the state, is to advocate the overthrow of organized government by unlawful means.'

* * * *

The precise question presented, and the only question which we can consider under this writ of error, then is, whether the statute, as construed and applied in this case, by the State courts, deprived the defendant of his liberty of expression in violation of the due process clause of the Fourteenth Amendment.

The statute does not penalize the utterance or publication of abstract "doctrine' or academic discussion having no quality of incitement to any concrete action. It is not aimed against mere historical or philosophical essays. It does not restrain the advocacy of changes in the form of government by constitutional and lawful means. What it prohibits is language advocating, advising or teaching the overthrow of organized government by unlawful means. These words imply urging to action.

* * * *

For present purposes we may and do assume that freedom of speech and of the press-which are protected by the First Amendment from abridgment by Congress-are among the fundamental personal rights and "liberties' protected by the due process clause of the Fourteenth Amendment from impairment by the States. * * *

(1) It is a fundamental principle, long established, that the freedom of speech and of the press which is secured by the Constitution, does not confer an absolute right to speak or publish, without responsibility, whatever one may choose, or an unrestricted and unbridled license that gives immunity for every possible use of language and prevents the punishment of those who abuse this freedom. * * *

2) That a State in the exercise of its police power may punish those who abuse this freedom by utterances inimical to the public wel-

fare, tending to corrupt public morals, incite to crime, or disturb the public peace, is not open to question. * * *

(3) And, for yet more imperative reasons, a State may punish utterances endangering the foundations of organized government and threatening its overthrow by unlawful means. These imperil its own existence as a constitutional State. * * *

(4, 5) By enacting the present statute the State has determined, through its legislative body, that utterances advocating the overthrow of organized government by force, violence and unlawful means, are so inimical to the general welfare and involve such danger of substantive evil that they may be penalized in the exercise of its police power. That determination must be given great weight. Every presumption is to be indulged in favor of the validity of the statute.

* * * *

6) We cannot hold that the present statute is an arbitrary or unreasonable exercise of the police power of the State unwarrantably infringing the freedom of speech or press; and we must and do sustain its constitutionality.

* * * *

The defendant's brief does not separately discuss any of the rulings of the trial court. It is only necessary to say that, applying the general rules already stated, we find that none of them involved any invasion of the constitutional rights of the defendant. It was not necessary, within the meaning of the statute, that the defendant should have advocated "some definite or immediate act or acts' of force, violence or unlawfulness. It was sufficient if such acts were advocated in general terms; and it was not essential that their immediate execution should have been advocated. Nor was it necessary that the language should have been "reasonably and ordinarily calculated to incite certain persons' to acts of force, violence or unlawfulness. The advocacy need not be addressed to specific persons. Thus, the publication and circulation of a newspaper article may be an encouragement or endeavor to persuade to murder, although not addressed to any person in particular.

We need not enter upon a consideration of the English common law rule of seditious libel or the Federal Sedition Act of 1798,11 to which reference is made in the defendant's brief. These are so unlike the present statute, that we think the decisions under them cast no helpful light upon the questions here.

And finding, for the reasons stated, that the statute is not in itself unconstitutional, and that it has not been applied in the present case in derogation of any constitutional right, the judgment of the Court of Appeals is Affirmed.

Decision

Affirmed.

Troy Leon **GREGG**
v.
State of **GEORGIA**
428 U.S. 153, 96 S.Ct. 2909, 49 L.Ed.2d 859
Argued March 31, 1976.
Decided July 2, 1976.
Stay Granted July 22, 1976.
Rehearing Denied Oct. 4, 1976.

Introduction

An Eighth Amendment/capital punishment case in which the Court indicated for the first time that the death penalty does not "invariably violate the Constitution."

WESTLAW Summary

Defendant was convicted in Georgia trial court of armed robbery and murder and was sentenced to death and he appealed. The Georgia Supreme Court affirmed except as to imposition of death sentence on robbery charges and certiorari was granted. The United States Supreme Court, Mr. Justice Stewart, Mr. Justice Powell, and Mr. Justice Stevens announcing the judgment of the court and filing an opinion delivered by Mr. Justice Stewart, held that punishment of death for the crime of murder did not, under all circumstances, violate the Eighth and Fourteenth Amendments; that retribution and the possibility of deterrence to capital crimes by prospective offenders were not impermissible considerations for legislature to weigh in determining whether the death penalty should be imposed; and that the Georgia statutory system under which the punishment and guilt portions of the trial are bifurcated, with the jury hearing additional evidence and argument before determining whether to impose death penalty, under which jury is instructed on statutory factors of aggravation and mitigation, and under which Georgia Supreme Court reviews each sentence of death to determine whether it is disproportionate to the punishment usually imposed in similar cases was constitutional despite contention that it permitted arbitrary and freakish imposition of the death penalty.

Case Excerpts

Judgment of the Court, and opinion of Mr. Justice STEWART, Mr. Justice POWELL, and Mr. Justice STEVENS, announced by Mr. Justice STEWART.

The issue in this case is whether the imposition of the sentence of death for the crime of murder under the law of Georgia violates the Eighth and Fourteenth Amendments.

The petitioner, Troy Gregg, was charged with committing armed robbery and murder. In accordance with Georgia procedure in capital cases, the trial was in two stages, a guilt stage and a sentencing stage. The evidence at the guilt trial established that on November 21, 1973, the petitioner and a traveling companion, Floyd Allen, while hitchhiking north in Florida were picked up by Fred Simmons and Bob Moore. Their car broke down, but they continued north after Simmons purchased another vehicle with some of the cash he was carrying. While still in Florida, they picked up another hitchhiker, Dennis Weaver, who rode with them to Atlanta, where he was let out about 11 p. m. A short time later the four men interrupted their journey for a rest stop along the highway. The next morning the bodies of Simmons and Moore were discovered in a ditch nearby.

* * * *

The trial judge submitted the murder charges to the jury on both felony-murder and nonfelony-murder theories. He also instructed on the issue of self-defense but declined to instruct on manslaughter. He submitted the robbery case to the jury on both an armed-robbery theory and on the lesser included offense of robbery by intimidation. The jury found the petitioner guilty of two counts of armed robbery and two counts of murder.

At the penalty stage, which took place before the same jury, neither the prosecutor nor the petitioner's lawyer offered any additional evidence. Both counsel, however, made lengthy arguments dealing generally with the propriety of capital punishment under the circumstances and with the weight of the evidence of guilt. The trial judge instructed the jury that it could recommend either a death sentence or a life prison sentence on each count. The judge further charged the jury that in determining what sentence was appropriate the jury was free to consider the facts and circumstances, if any, presented by the parties in mitigation or aggravation.

* * * *

The Supreme Court of Georgia affirmed the convictions and the imposition of the death sentences for murder. After reviewing the trial transcript and the record, including the evidence, and comparing the evidence and sentence in similar cases in accordance with the requirements of Georgia law, the court concluded that, considering the nature of the crime and the defendant, the sentences of death had not resulted from prejudice or any other arbitrary factor and were not excessive or disproportionate to the penalty applied in similar cases. The death sentences used for armed robbery, however, were vacated on the grounds that the death penalty had rarely been imposed in Georgia for that offense and that the jury improperly considered the murders as aggravating circumstances for the robberies after having considered the armed robberies as aggravating circumstances for the murders.

* * * *

The Court on a number of occasions has both assumed and asserted the constitutionality of capital punishment. In several cases that assumption provided a necessary foundation for the decision, as the Court was asked to decide whether a particular method of carrying out a capital sentence would be allowed to stand under the Eighth Amendment. But until Furman v. Georgia (citation omitted), the Court never confronted squarely the fundamental claim that the punishment of death always, regardless of the enormity of the offense or the procedure followed in imposing the sentence, is cruel and unusual punishment in violation of the Constitution. Although this issue was presented and addressed in Furman, it was not resolved by the Court. * * *

* * * *

It is apparent from the text of the Constitution itself that the existence of capital punishment was accepted by the Framers. At the time the Eighth Amendment was ratified, capital punishment was a common sanction in every State. * * *

Cruel and unusual punishments are forbidden by the Constitution, but the authorities referred to are quite sufficient to show that the punishment of shooting as a mode of executing the death penalty for the crime of murder in the first degree is not included in that category, within the meaning of the eighth amendment."

* * * *

The petitioners in the capital cases before the Court today renew the "standards of decency" argument, but developments during the four years since Furman Have undercut substantially the assumptions upon which their argument rested. Despite the continuing debate, dating back to the 19th century, over the morality and utility of capital punishment, it is now evident that a large proportion of American society continues to regard it as an appropriate and necessary criminal sanction.

* * * *

In sum, we cannot say that the judgment of the Georgia Legislature that capital punishment may be necessary in some cases is clearly wrong. Considerations of federalism, as well as respect for the ability of a legislature to evaluate, in terms of its particular State, the moral consensus concerning the death penalty and its social utility as a sanction, require us to conclude, in the absence of more convincing evidence, that the infliction of dea as a punishment for murder is not without justification and thus is not unconstitutionally severe.

* * * *

Furman mandates that where discretion is afforded a sentencing body on a matter so grave as the determination of whether a human life should be taken or spared, that discretion must be suitably directed and limited so as to minimize the risk of wholly arbitrary and capricious action.

* * * *

In summary, the concerns expressed in Furman that the penalty of death not be imposed in an arbitrary or capricious manner can be met by a carefully drafted statute that ensures that the sentencing authority is given adequate information and guidance. As a general proposition these concerns are best met by a system that provides for a bifurcated proceeding at which the sentencing authority is apprised of the information relevant to the imposition of sentence and provided with standards to guide its use of the information.

* * * *

We now turn to consideration of the constitutionality of Georgia's capital-sentencing procedures. In the wake of Furman, Georgia amended its capital punishment statute, but chose not to narrow the scope of its murder provisions. * * * Thus, now as before Furman, in Georgia "(a) person commits murder when he unlawfully and with malice aforethought, either express or implied, causes the death of another human being." All persons convicted of murder "shall be punished by death or by imprisonment for life."

* * * *

In short, Georgia's new sentencing procedures require as a prerequisite to the imposition of the death penalty, specific jury findings as to the circumstances of the crime or the character of the defendant. Moreover, to guard further against a situation comparable to that presented in Furman, the Supreme Court of Georgia compares each death sentence with the sentences imposed on similarly situated defendants to ensure that the sentence of death in a particular case is not disproportionate. On their face these procedures seem to satisfy the concerns of Furman. No longer should there be "no meaningful basis for distinguishing the few cases in which (the death penalty) is imposed from the many cases in which it is not."

* * * *

For the reasons expressed in this opinion, we hold that the statutory system under which Gregg was sentenced to death does not violate the Constitution. Accordingly, the judgment of the Georgia Supreme Court is affirmed.

Decision

Affirmed.

KAISER ALUMINUM AND CHEMICAL CO. (United Steelworkers of America, AFL-CIO-CLC)
v.
Brian F. **WEBER** et al.
443 U.S. 193, 99 S.Ct. 2721, 61 L.Ed.2d 480
Argued March 28, 1979.
Decided June 27, 1979.

Introduction

A civil rights/reverse discrimination case in which a union apprenticeship program that used a racial quota was deemed legal even if it violated the words of the Civil Rights Act of 1964 because it did not violate the spirit. Essentially, any form of reverse discrimination—even explicit quotas—is permissible provided that it is the result of legislative, executive, or judicial findings of past discrimination.

WESTLAW Summary

White employee brought action against employer and union challenging legality of plan for on-the-job training which mandated a one-for-one quota for minority workers admitted to the program. The United States District Court for the Eastern District of Louisiana enjoined operation of the agreement and employer and union appealed. The Court of Appeals affirmed, and certiorari was granted. The Supreme Court held that: (1) Title VII's prohibitions against racial discrimination does not condemn all private, voluntary, race-conscious affirmative action plans, and (2) an affirmative action plan that was collectively bargained by an employer and a union and that reserved for black employees 50 percent of the openings in an in-plant craft training program until the percentage of black craft workers in plant was commensurate with the percentage of blacks in the local labor force did not violate Title VII's prohibition against racial discrimination; the purposes of the plan mirrored those of the statute, the plan did not unnecessarily trammel the interests of white employees, and the plan was a temporary measure, not intended to maintain racial balance, but simply to eliminate a manifest racial imbalance.

Case Excerpts

Mr. Justice BRENNAN delivered the opinion of the Court.

Challenged here is the legality of an affirmative action plan-collectively bargained by an employer and a union-that reserves for black employees 50% of the openings in an in-plant craft-training program until the percentage of black craft-workers in the plant is commensurate with the percentage of blacks in the local labor force. The question for decision is whether Congress, in Title VII of the Civil Rights Act of 1964, left employers and unions in the private sector free to take such race-conscious steps to eliminate manifest racial imbalances in traditionally segregated job categories. We hold that Title VII does not prohibit such race-conscious affirmative action plans.

In 1974, petitioner United Steelworkers of America (USWA) and petitioner Kaiser Aluminum & Chemical Corp. (Kaiser) entered into a master collective-bargaining agreement covering terms and conditions of employment at 15 Kaiser plants. The agreement contained, inter alia, an affirmative action plan designed to eliminate conspicuous racial imbalances in Kaiser's then almost exclusively white craft-work forces. Black craft-hiring goals were set for each Kaiser plant equal to the percentage of blacks in the respective local labor forces. To enable plants to meet these goals, on-the-job training programs were established to teach unskilled production workers-black and white-the skills necessary to become craftworkers. The plan reserved for black employees 50% of the openings in these newly created in-plant training programs.

(1) This case arose from the operation of the plan at Kaiser's plant in Gramercy, La. Until 1974, Kaiser hired as craftworkers for that plant only persons who had had prior craft experience. Because blacks had long been excluded from craft unions,1 few were able to present such credentials. As a consequence, prior to 1974 only 1.83% (5 out of 273) of the skilled craftworkers at the Gramercy plant were black, even though the work force in the Gramercy area was approximately 39% black.

Pursuant to the national agreement Kaiser altered its craft-hiring practice in the Gramercy plant. Rather than hiring already trained outsiders, Kaiser established a training program to train its production workers to fill craft openings. Selection of craft trainees was made on the basis of seniority, with the proviso that at least 50% of the new trainees were to be black until the percentage of black skilled craftworkers in the Gramercy plant approximated the percentage of blacks in the local labor force.

During 1974, the first year of the operation of the Kaiser-USWA affirmative action plan, 13 craft trainees were selected from Gramercy's production work force. Of these, seven were black and six white. The most senior black selected into the program had less seniority than several white production workers whose bids for admission were rejected. Thereafter one of those white production workers, respondent Brian Weber (hereafter respondent), instituted this class action in the United States District Court for the Eastern District of Louisiana.

* * * *

Respondent argues that Congress intended in Title VII to prohibit all ra ce-conscious affirmative action plans. Respondent's argument rests upon a literal interpretation of sections 703(a) and (d) of the Act. Those sections make it unlawful to "discriminate . . . because of . . . race" in hiring and in the selection of apprentices for training programs. * * *

Respondent's argument is not without force. But it overlooks the significance of the fact that the Kaiser-USWA plan is an affirmative action plan voluntarily adopted by private parties to eliminate traditional patterns of racial segregation. * * * The prohibition against racial discrimination in sections 703(a) and (d) of Title VII must therefore be read against the background of the legislative history of Title VII and the historical context from which the Act arose. Examination of those sources makes clear that an interpretation of the sections that forbade all race-conscious affirmative action would "bring about an end completely at variance with the purpose of the statute" and must be rejected.

Congress' primary concern in enacting the prohibition against racial discrimination in Title VII of the Civil Rights Act of 1964 was with "the plight of the Negro in our economy." (citation omitted)

Before 1964, blacks were largely relegated to "unskilled and semi-skilled jobs." (citation omitted) Because of automation the number of such jobs was rapidly decreasing. As a consequence, "the relative position of the Negro worker (was) steadily worsening. In 1947 the non-white unemployment rate was only 64 percent higher than the white rate; in 1962 it was 124 percent higher." (citation omitted) Congress considered this a serious social problem. * * *

* * * *

Congress feared that the goals of the Civil Rights Act-the integration of blacks into the mainstream of American society-could not be achieved unless this trend were reversed. And Congress recognized that that would not be possible unless blacks were able to secure jobs "which have a future." (citation omitted) * * *

* * * *

Given this legislative history, we cannot agree with respondent that Congress intended to prohibit the private sector from taking effective steps to accomplish the goal that Congress designed Title VII to achieve. The very statutory words intended as a spur or catalyst to cause "employers and unions to self-examine and to self-evaluate their employment practices and to endeavor to eliminate, so far as possible, the last vestiges of an unfortunate and ignominious page in this country's history," (citation omitted) cannot be interpreted as an absolute prohibition against all private, voluntary, race-conscious affirmative action efforts to hasten the elimination of such vestiges. It would be ironic indeed if a law triggered by a Nation's concern over centuries of racial injustice and intended to improve the lot of those who had "been excluded from the American dream for so long," constituted the first legislative prohibition of all voluntary, private, race-conscious efforts to abolish traditional patterns of racial segregation and hierarchy.

Our conclusion is further reinforced by examination of the language and legislative history of section 703(j) of Title VII. Opponents of Title VII raised two related arguments against the bill. First, they argued that the Act would be interpreted to require employers with racially imbalanced work forces to grant preferential treatment to racial minorities in order to integrate. Second, they argued that employers with racially imbalanced work forces would grant preferential treatment to racial minorities, even if not required to do so by the Act. Had Congress meant to prohibit all race-conscious affirmative action,

as respondent urges, it easily could have answered both objections by providing that Title VII would not require or permit racially preferential integration efforts. But Congress did not choose such a course.
* * *

We therefore hold that Title VII's prohibition in sections 703(a) and (d) against racial discrimination does not condemn all private, voluntary, race-conscious affirmative action plans.

* * * *

We conclude, therefore, that the adoption of the Kaiser-USWA plan for the Gramercy plant falls within the area of discretion left by Title VII to the private sector voluntarily to adopt affirmative action plans designed to eliminate conspicuous racial imbalance in traditionally segregated job categories. * * *

Decision

Reversed.

Charles **KATZ**
v.
UNITED STATES
389 U.S. 347, 88 S.Ct. 507, 19 L.Ed.2d 576
Argued Oct. 17, 1967.
Decided Dec. 18, 1967.

Introduction

A Fourth Amendment/wiretapping case in which the Court overturned Katz' conviction for transmitting betting information across state lines from a public phone booth in Los Angeles. The FBI had placed recording devices outside the booth without a warrant.

WESTLAW Summary

Defendant was convicted in the United States District Court for the Southern District of California, Central Division, of a violation of statute proscribing interstate transmission by wire communication of bets or wagers, and he appealed. The Court of Appeals affirmed, and certiorari was granted. The Supreme Court held that government's activities in electronically listening to and recording defendant's words spoken into telephone receiver in public telephone booth violated the privacy upon which defendant justifiably relied while using the telephone booth and thus constituted a "search and seizure' within Fourth Amendment, and the fact that the electronic device employed to achieve that end did not happen to penetrate the wall of the booth could have no constitutional significance. The Court further held that the search and seizure, without prior judicial sanction and attendant safeguards, did not comply with constitutional standards, although, in accepting the account of the government's actions as accurate, the magistrate could constitutionally have authorized with appropriate safeguards the very limited search and seizure that the government asserted in fact took place and although it was apparent that the agents had acted with restraint.

Case Excerpts

MR. JUSTICE STEWART delivered the opinion of the Court.

The petitioner was convicted in the District Court for the Southern District of California under an eight-count indictment charging him with transmitting wagering information by telephone from Los Angeles to Miami and Boston in violation of a federal statute. At trial the Government was permitted, over the petitioner's objection, to introduce evidence of the petitioner's end of telephone coversations, overheard by FBI agents who had attached an electronic listening and recording device to the outside of the public telephone booth from which he had placed his calls. In affirming his conviction, the Court of Appeals rejected the contention that the recordings had been obtained in violation of the Fourth Amendment, because "(t)here was no physical entrance into the area occupied by, (the petitioner).' We granted certiorari in order to consider the constitutional questions thus presented.

* * * *

Because of the misleading way the issues have been formulated, the parties have attached great significance to the characterization of the telephone booth from which the petitioner placed his calls. The petitioner has strenuously argued that the booth was a "constitutionally protected area.' The Government has maintained with equal vigor that it was not. But this effort to decide whether or not a given "area,' viewed in the abstract, is "constitutionally protected' deflects attention from the problem presented by this case. For the Fourth Amendment protects people, not places. What a person knowingly exposes to the public, even in his own home or office, is not a subject of Fourth Amendment protection. But what he seeks to preserve as private, even in an area accessible to the public, may be constitutionally protected.

The Government stresses the fact that the telephone booth from which the petitioner made his calls was constructed partly of glass, so that he was as visible after he entered it as he would have been if he had remained outside. But what he sought to exclude when he entered the booth was not the intruding eye-it was the uninvited ear. He did not shed his right to do so simply because he made his calls from a place where he might be seen. * * * One who occupies [the telephone booth], shuts the door behind him, and pays the toll that permits him to place a call is surely entitled to assume that the words he utters into the mouthpiece will not be broadcast to the world. To read the Constitution more narrowly is to ignore the vital role that the public telephone has come to play in private communication.

The Government contends, however, tha the activities of its agents in this case should not be tested by Fourth Amendment requirements, for the surveillance technique they employed involved no physical penetration of the telephone booth from which the petitioner placed his calls. It is true that the absence of such penetration was at one time thought to foreclose further Fourth Amendment inquiry for that Amendment was thought to limit only searches and seizures of tangible property. But "(t)he premise that property interests control the right of the Government to search and seize has been discredited.' * * * (citation omitted) [We] have expressly held that the Fourth Amendment governs not only the seizure of tangible items, but extends as well to the recording of oral statements overheard without any "technical trespass under * * * local property law.' (citation omitted) Once this much is acknowledged, and once it is recognized that the Fourth Amendment protects people-and not simply "areas'-against unreasonable searches and seizures it becomes clear that the reach of that Amendment cannot trun upon the presence or absence of a physical intrusion into any given enclosure.

* * * *

The question remaining for decision, then, is whether the search and seizure conducted in this case complied with constitutional standards. In that regard, the Government's position is that its agents acted in an entirely defensible manner: They did not begin their electronic surveillance until investigation of the petitioner's activities had established a strong probability that he was using the telephone in question to transmit gambling information to persons in other States, in violation of federal law. Moreover, the surveillance was limited, both in scope and in duration, to the specific purpose of establishing the contents of the petitioner's unlawful telephonic communications. The agents confined their surveillance to the brief periods during which he used the telephone booth, and they took great care to overhear only the conversations of the petitioner himself.

Accepting this account of the Government's actions as acccurate, it is clear that this surveillance was so narrowly circumscribed that a duly authorized magistrate, properly notified of the need for such investigation, specifically informed of the basis on which it was to proceed, and clearly apprised of the precise intrusion it would entail, could constitutionally have authorized, with appropriate safeguards, the very limited search and seizure that the Government asserts in fact took place. * * *

The Government urges that, because * * * they did no more here than they might properly have done with prior judicial sanction, we should retroactively validate their conduct. That we cannot do. It is apparent that the agents in this case acted with restraint. Yet the inescapable fact is that this restraint was imposed by the agents themselves, not by a judicial officer. They were not required, before commencing the search, to present their estimate of probable cause for detached scrutiny by a neutral magistrate. They were not compelled, during the conduct of the search itself, to observe precise limits established in advance by a specific court order. Nor were they directed, after the search had been completed, to notify the authorizing magistrate in detail of all that had been seized. In the absence of such safeguards, this Court has never sustained a search upon the sole ground that officers reasonably expected to find evidence of a particular crime and voluntarily confined their activities to the least intrusive means consistent with that end.

* * * *

* * * Wherever a man may be, he is entitled to know that he will remain free from unreasonable searches and seizures. The government agents here ignored "the procedure of antecedent justification * * * that is central to the Fourth Amendment,'a procedure that we hold to be a constitutional precondition of the kind of electronic surveillance involved in this case. Because the surveillance here failed to meet that condition, and because it led to the petitioner's conviction, the judgment must be reversed.

It is so ordered.

Decision

Judgment reversed.

Dollree **MAPP**, etc.
v.
OHIO.
367 U.S. 643, 81 S.Ct. 1684, 6 L.Ed.2d 1081
Argued March 29, 1961.
Decided June 19, 1961.
Rehearing Denied Oct. 9, 1961.

Introduction

A rights of the accused/exclusionary-rule case in which the Court overturned the conviction of Dollree Mapp for possession of obscene materials because police had found pornographic books in her apartment after searching it without a warrant despite her verbal refusal to let them in.

WESTLAW Summary

Prosecution for possession and control of obscene material. An Ohio Common Pleas Court rendered judgment, and the defendant appealed. The Ohio Supreme Court affirmed the judgment, and the defendant again appealed. The Supreme Court held that evidence obtained by unconstitutional search was inadmissible and vitiated conviction.

Reversed and remanded.

Case Excerpts

Mr. Justice CLARK delivered the opinion of the Court.

Appellant stands convicted of knowingly having had in her possession and under her control certain lewd and lascivious books, pictures, and photographs in violation of s 2905.34 of Ohio's Revised Code. As officially stated in the syllabus to its opinion, the Supreme Court of Ohio found that her conviction was valid though "based primarily upon the introduction in evidence of lewd and lascivious books and pictures unlawfully seized during an unlawful search of defendant's home * * *.' (citation omitted)

On May 23, 1957, three Cleveland police officers arrived at appellant's residence in that city pursuant to information that "a person (was) hiding out in the home, who was wanted for questioning in connection with a recent bombing, and that there was a large amount of policy paraphernalia being hidden in the home.' Miss Mapp and her daughter by a former marriage lived on the top floor of the two-family dwelling. Upon their arrival at that house, the officers knocked on the door and demanded entrance but appellant, after telephoning her attorney, refused to admit them without a search warrant. They advised their headquarters of the situation and undertook a surveillance of the house.

The officers again sought entrance some three hours later when four or more additional officers arrived on the scene. When Miss Mapp did not come to the door immediately, at least one of the several doors to the house was forcibly opened and the policemen gained admittance. Meanwhile Miss Mapp's attorney arrived, but the officers, having secured their own entry, and continuing in their defiance of the law, would permit him neither to see Miss Mapp nor to enter the house. It appears that Miss Mapp was halfway down the stairs from the upper floor to the front door when the officers, in this highhanded manner, broke into the hall. She demanded to see the search warrant. * * * A struggle ensued in which the officers recovered the piece of paper and as a result of which they handcuffed appellant because she had been "belligerent' in resisting their official rescue of the "warrant' from her person. Running roughshod over appellant, a policeman "grabbed' her, "twisted (her) hand,' and she "yelled (and) pleaded with him' because "it was hurting.' Appellant, in handcuffs, was then forcibly taken upstairs to her bedroom where the officers searched a dresser, a chest of drawers, a closet and some suitcases. They also looked into a photo album and through personal papers belonging to the appellant. The search spread to the rest of the second floor including the child's bedroom, the living room, the kitchen and a dinette. The basement of the building and a trunk found therein were also searched. The obscene materials for possession of which she was ultimately convicted were discovered in the course of that widespread search.

At the trial no search warrant was produced by the prosecution, nor was the failure to produce one explained or accounted for. At best, "There is, in the record, considerable doubt as to whether there ever was any warrant for the search of defendant's home.' The Ohio Supreme Court believed a "reasonable argument' could be made that the conviction should be reversed "because the "methods' employed to obtain the (evidence) were such as to "offend "a sense of justice,"' but the court found determinative the fact that the evidence had not been taken "from defendant's person by the use of brutal or offensive physical force against defendant.'

The State says that even if the search were made without authority, or otherwise unreasonably, it is not prevented from usin g the unconstitutionally seized evidence at trial * * *.

* * * [T]he doctrines of [the Fifth and Fourteenth] Amendments 'apply to all invasions on the part of the government and its employees of the sanctity of a man's home and the privacies of life. It is not the breaking of his doors, and the rummaging of his drawers, that constitutes the essence of the offence; but it is the invasion of his indefeasible right of personal security, personal liberty and private property * * *. Breaking into a house and opening boxes and drawers are circumstances of aggravation; but any forcible and compulsory extortion of a man's own testimony or of his private papers to be used as evidence to convict him of crime or to forfeit his goods, is within the condemnation * * * (of those Amendments).'

* * * *

* * * [The] 4th Amendment * * * put the courts of the United States and Federal officials, in the exercise of their power and authority, under limitations and restraints (and) * * * forever secure(d) the people, their persons, houses, papers, and effects, against all unreasonable searches and seizures under the guise of law * * * and the duty of giving to it force and effect is obligatory upon all entrusted under our Federal system with the enforcement of the laws.'

Specifically dealing with the use of the evidence unconstitutionally seized, the Court concluded:

"If letters and private documents can thus be seized and held and used in evidence against a citizen accused of an offense, the protection of the Fourth Amendment declaring his right to be secure against such searches and seizures is of no value, and, so far as those thus placed are concerned, might as well be stricken from the Constitution. The efforts of the courts and their officials to bring the guilty to punishment, praiseworthy as they are, are not to be aided by the sacrifice of those great principles established by years of endeavor and suffering which have resulted in their embodiment in the fundamental law of the land.' (citation omitted)

* * * *

Since the Fourth Amendment's right of privacy has been declared enforceable against the States through the Due Process Clause of the Fourteenth, it is enforceable against them by the same sanction of exclusion as is used against the Federal Government. Were it otherwise, then * * * the assurance against unreasonable federal searches and seizures would be "a form of words', valueless and undeserving of mention in a perpetual charter of inestimable human liberties, so too, without that rule the freedom from state invasions of privacy would be so epemeral and so neatly severed from its conceptual nexus with the freedom from all brutish means of coercing evidence as not to merit this Court's high regard as a freedom "implicit in "the concept of ordered liberty." * * * To hold otherwise is to grant the right but in reality to withhold its privilege and enjoyment. Only last year the Court itself recognized that the purpose of the exclusionary rule "is to deter-to compel respect for the constitutional guaranty in the only effectively available way-by removing the incentive to disregard it.' (citation omitted). Indeed, we are aware of no restraint, similar to that rejected today, conditioning the enforcement of any other basic constitutional right. The right to privacy, no less important than any other right carefully and particularly reserved to the people, would stand in marked contrast to all other rights declared as "basic to a free society.' (citation omitted) This Court has not hesitated to enforce as strictly against the States as it does against the Federal Government the rights of free speech and of a free press, the rights to notice and to a fair, public trial, including, as it does, the right not to be convicted by use of a coerced confession, however logically relevant it be, and without regard to its reliability.

* * * *

Moreover, our holding that the exclusionary rule is an essential part of both the Fourth and Fourteenth Amendments is not only the logical dictate of prior cases, but it also makes very good sense. There is no war between the Constitution and common sense. Presently, a federal prosecutor may make no use of evidence illegally seized, but a State's attorney across the street may, although he supposedly is operating under the enforceable prohibitions of the same Amendment. Thus the State, by admitting evidence unlawfully seized, serves to encourage disobedience to the Federal Constitution which it is bound to uphold.

* * * *

* * * Having once recognized that the right to privacy embodied in the Fourth Amendment is enforceable against the States, and that the right to be secure against rude invasions of privacy by state officers is, therefore, constitutional in origin, we can no longer permit that right to remain an empty promise. Because it is enforceable in the same manner and to like effect as other basic rights secured by the Due Process Clause, we can no longer permit it to be revocable at the whim of any police officer who, in the name of law enforcement itself, chooses to suspend its enjoyment. Our decision, founded on reason and truth, gives to the individual no more than that which the Constitution guarantees him, to the police officer no less than that to which honest law enforcement is entitled, and, to the courts, that judicial integrity so necessary in the true administration of justice.

The judgment of the Supreme Court of Ohio is reversed and the cause remanded for further proceedings not inconsistent with this opinion.

Decision

Reversed and remanded.

Marvin **MILLER**
v.
State of **CALIFORNIA**.
413 U.S. 15, 93 S.Ct. 2607, 37 L.Ed.2d 419
Argued Jan. 18-19, 1972.
Reargued Nov. 7, 1972.
Decided June 21, 1973.
Rehearing Denied Oct. 9, 1973.

Introduction

A freedom of speech/obscenity case in which the Court created a formal list of requirements as a test of obscenity that must be meet for material to be legally obscene. They are that (1) the average person finds that it violates contemporary community standards, (2) the work taken as a whole appeals to prurient interest in sex, (3) the work shows patently offensive sexual conduct, and (4) the work lacks serious redeeming literary, artistic, political, or scientific merit.

WESTLAW Summary

Defendant was convicted of mailing unsolicited sexually explicit material in violation of a California statute and the Appellate Department, Superior Court of California, County of Orange, affirmed and defendant appealed. The Supreme Court held that a work may be subject to state regulation where that work, taken as a whole, appeals to the prurient interest in sex; portrays, in a patently offensive way, sexual conduct specifically defined by the applicable state law; and, taken as a whole, does not have serious literary, artistic, political or scientific value. The Court also rejected the test of "utterly without redeeming social value' as a constitutional standard.

Case Excerpts

Mr. Chief Justice BURGER delivered the opinion of the Court.

* * * *

Appellant conducted a mass mailing campaign to advertise the sale of illustrated books, euphemistically called "adult' material. After a jury trial, he was convicted of violating California Penal Code s 311.2(a), a misdemeanor, by knowingly distributing obscene matter, and the Appellate Department, Superior Court of California, County of Orange, summarily affirmed the judgment without opinion. Appellant's conviction was specifically based on his conduct in causing five unsolicited advertising brochures to be sent through the mail in an envelope addressed to a restaurant in Newport Beach, California. The envelope was opened by the manager of the restaurant and his mother. They had not requested the brochures; they complained to the police.

* * * *

This case involves the application of a State's criminal obscenity statute to a situation in which sexually explicit materials have been thrust by aggressive sales action upon unwilling recipients who had in no way indicated any desire to receive such materials. This Court has recognized that the States have a legitimate interest in prohibiting dissemination or exhibition of obscene material when the mode of dissemination carries with it a significant danger of offending the sensibilities of unwilling recipients or of exposure to juveniles. It is in this context that we are called on to define the standards which must be used to identify obscene material that a State may regulate without infringing on the First Amendment as applicable to the States through the Fourteenth Amendment.

* * * *

"* * * There are certain well-defined and narrowly limited classes of speech, the prevention and punishment of which have never been thought to raise any Constitutional problem. These include the lewd and obscene . . . . It has been well observed that such utterances are no essential part of any exposition of ideas, and are of such slight social value as a step to truth that any benefit that may be derived from them is clearly outweighed by the social interest in order and morality . . . .' (citation omitted)

This much has been categorically settled by the Court, that obscene material is unprotected by the First Amendment. We acknowledge, however, the inherent dangers of undertaking to regulate any form of expression. State statutes designed to regulate obscene materials must be carefully limited. As a result, we now confine the permissible scope of such regulation to works which depict or describe sexual conduct. That conduct must be specifically defined by the applicable state law, as written or authoritatively construed. A state offense must also be limited to works which, taken as a whole, appeal to the prurient interest in sex, which portray sexual conduct in a patently offensive way, and which, taken as a whole, do not have serious literary, artistic, political, or scientific value.

The basic guidelines for the trier of fact must be: (a) whether "the average person, applying contemporary community standards' would find that the work, taken as a whole, appeals to the prurient interest; (b) whether the work depicts or describes, in a patently offensive way, sexual conduct specifically defined by the applicable state law; and (c) whether the work, taken as a whole, lacks serious literary, artistic, political, or scientific value. (citations omitted) * * *

Under the holdings announced today, no one will be subject to prosecution for the sale or exposure of obscene materials unless these materials depict or describe patently offensive "hard core' sexual conduct specifically defined by the regulating state law, as written or construed. We are satisfied that these specific prerequisites will provide fair notice to a dealer in such materials that his public and commercial activities may bring prosecution. If the inability to define regulated materials with ultimate, god-like precision altogether removes the power of the States or the Congress to regulate, then "hard core' pornography may be exposed without limit to the juvenile, the passerby, and the consenting adult alike * * *.

* * * *

Under a National Constitution, fundamental First Amendment limitations on the powers of the States do not vary from community to community, but this does not mean that there are, or should or can be, fixed, uniform national standards of precisely what appeals to the "prurient interest' or is "patently offensive.' These are essentially questions of fact, and our Nation is simply too big and too diverse for this Court to reasonably expect that such standards could be articulated for all 50 States in a single formulation, even assuming the prerequisite consensus exists. When triers of fact are asked to decide whether "the average person, applying contemporary community standards' would consider certain materials "prurient,' it would be unrealistic to require that the answer be based on some abstract formulation. The adversary system, with lay jurors as the usual ultimate factfinders in criminal prosecutions, has historically permitted triers of fact to draw on the standards of their community, guided always by limiting instructions on the law. To require a State to structure obscenity proceedings around evidence of a national "community standard' would be an exercise in futility.

* * * *

In sum, we (a) reaffirm * * * that obscene material is not protected by the First Amendment; (b) hold that such material can be regulated by the States, subject to the specific safeguards enunciated above, without a showing that the material is "utterly without redeeming social value'; and (c) hold that obscenity is to be determined by applying "contemporary community standards,' not "national standards.' The judgment of the Appellate Department of the Superior Court, Orange County, California, is vacated and the case remanded to that court for further proceedings not inconsistent with the First Amendment standards established by this opinion.

Decision

Vacated and remanded.

Ernesto A. **MIRANDA**
v.
State of **ARIZONA.**
384 U.S. 436, 86 S.Ct. 1602, 16 L.Ed.2d 694
Argued Feb. 28, 1966.
Decided June 13, 1966.

Introduction

A rights of the accused/right to remain silent case in which a mentally disturbed suspect, Ernesto Miranda, had been arrested, questioned for two hours, and confessed to the crime of kidnapping and rape. His conviction was reversed by the Supreme Court on the basis of the Fifth and Sixth Amendments. Now people are read their "Miranda rights" which include the right to remain silent.

WESTLAW Summary

Criminal prosecution. The Superior Court, Maricopa County, Arizona, rendered judgment, and the Supreme Court of Arizona affirmed. The defendant obtained certiorari. The Supreme Court held that statements obtained from defendants during incommunicado interrogation in police-dominated atmosphere, without full warning of constitutional rights, were inadmissible as having been obtained in violation of Fifth Amendment privilege against self-incrimination.

Case Excerpts

Mr. Chief Justice WARREN delivered the opinion of the Court.

[On March 13, 1963, petitioner, Ernesto Miranda, was arrested at his home and taken in custody to a Phoenix police station. He was there identified by the complaining witness. The police then took him to "Interrogation Room No. 2' of the detective bureau. There he was questioned by two police officers. The officers admitted at trial that Miranda was not advised that he had a right to have an attorney present. Two hours later, the officers emerged from the interrogation room with a written confession signed by Miranda. At the top of the statement was a typed paragraph stating that the confession was made voluntarily, without threats or promises of immunity and "with full knowledge of my legal rights, understanding any statement I make may be used against me.'

At his trial before a jury, the written confession was admitted into evidence over the objection of defense counsel, and the officers testified to the prior oral confession made by Miranda during the interrogation. Miranda was found guilty of kidnapping and rape. He was sentenced to 20 to 30 years' imprisonment on each count, the sentences to run concurrently. On appeal, the Supreme Court of Arizona held that Miranda's constitutional rights were not violated in obtaining the confession and affirmed the conviction. In reaching its decision, the court emphasized heavily the fact that Miranda did not specifically request counsel.]

The case before us raise questions which go to the roots of our concepts of American criminal jurisprudence: the restraints society must observe consistent with the Federal Constitution in prosecuting individuals for crime. More specifically, we deal with the admissibility of statements obtained from an individual who is subjected to custodial police interrogation and the necessity for procedures which accure that the individual is accorded his privilege under the Fifth Amendment to the Constitution not to be compelled to incriminate himself.

* * * *

* * * While the admissions or confessions of the prisoner, when voluntarily and freely made, have always ranked high in the scale of incriminating evidence, if an accused person be asked to explain his apparent connection with a crime under investigation, the ease with which the questions put to him may assume an inquisitorial character, the temptation to press the witness unduly, to browbeat him if he be timid or reluctant, to push him into a corner, and to entrap him into fatal contradictions, wh ich is so painfully evident in many of the earlier state trials * * *.

* * * *

Our holding will be spelled out with some specificity in the pages which follow but briefly stated it is this: the prosecution may not use statements, whether exculpatory or inculpatory, stemming from custodial interrogation of the defendant unless it demonstrates the use of procedural safeguards effective to secure the privilege against self-incrimination. By custodial interrogation, we mean questioning initiated by law enforcement officers after a person has been taken into custody or otherwise deprived of his freedom of action in any significant way. As for the procedural safeguards to be employed, unless other fully effective means are devised to inform accused persons of their right of silence and to assure a continuous opportunity to exercise it, the following measures are required. Prior to any questioning, the person must be warned that he has a right to remain silent, that any statement he does make may be used as evidence against him, and that he has a right to the presence of an attorney, either retained or appointed. The defendant may waive effectuation of these rights, provided the waiver is made voluntarily, knowingly and intelligently. If, however, he indicates in any manner and at any stage of the process that he wishes to consult with an attorney before speaking there can be no questioning. Likewise, if the individual is alone and indicates in any manner that he does not wish to be interrogated, the police may not question him. The mere fact that he may have answered some questions or volunteered some statements on his own does not deprive him of the right to refrain from answering any further inquiries until he has consulted with an attorney and thereafter consents to be questioned.

* * * *

In [this case], we might not find the defendant's statements to have been involuntary in traditional terms. Our concern for adequate safeguards to protect precious Fifth Amendment rights is, of course, not lessened in the slightest. In each of the cases, the defendant was thrust into an unfamiliar atmosphere and run through menacing police interrogation procedures. The potentiality for compulsion is forcefully apparent [in this case] where the indigent Mexican defendant was a seriously disturbed individual with pronounced sexual fantasies * * *. To be sure, the records do not evince overt physical coercion or patent psychological ploys. The fact remains that * * * the officers [did not] undertake to afford appropriate safeguards at the outset of the interrogation to insure that the statements were truly the product of free choice.

It is obvious that such an interrogation environment is created for no purpose other than to subjugate the individual to the will of his examiner. This atmosphere carries its own badge of intimidation. To be sure, this is not physical intimidation, but it is equally destructive of human dignity. The current practice of incommunicado interrogation is at odds with one of our Nation's most cherished principles-that the individual may not be compelled to incriminate himself. Unless adequate protective devices are employed to dispel the compulsion inherent in custodial surroundings, no statement obtained from the defendant can truly be the product of his free choice. * * *

* * * *

The question in [this case] is whether the privilege is fully applicable during a period of custodial interrogation. In this Court, the privilege has consistently been accorded a liberal construction. We are satisfied that all the principles embodied in the privilege apply to informal compulsion exerted by law-enforcement officers during in-custody questioning. An individual swept from familiar surroundings into police custody, surrounded by antagonistic forces, and subjected to the techniques of persuasion described above cannot be otherwise than under compulsion to speak. As a practical matter, the compulsion to speak in the isolated setting of the police station may well be greater than in courts or other official investigations, where there are often impartial observers to guard against intimidation or trickery.

* * * *

Today, then, there can be no doubt that the Fifth Amendment privilege is available outside of criminal court proceedings and serves to protect persons in all settings in which their freedom of action is curtailed in any significant way from being compelled to incriminate themselves. We have concluded that without proper safeguards the process of in-custody interrogation of persons suspected or accused of crime contains inherently compelling pressures which work to undermine the individual's will to resist and to compel him to speak where he would not otherwise do so freely. In order to combat these pre ssures and to permit a full opportunity to exercise the privilege against self-incrimination, the accused must be adequately and effectively apprised of his rights and the exercise of those rights must be fully honored.

* * * *

To summarize, we hold that when an individual is taken into custody or otherwise deprived of his freedom by the authorities in any significant way and is subjected to questioning, the privilege against self-incrimination is jeopardized. Procedural safeguards must be employed to protect the privilege and unless other fully effective means are adopted to notify the person of his right of silence and to assure that the exercise of the right will be scrupulously honored, the following measures are required. He must be warned prior to any questioning that he has the right to remain silent, that anything he says can be used against him in a court of law, that he has the right to the presence of an attorney, and that if he cannot afford an attorney one will be appointed for him prior to any questioning if he so desires. Opportunity to exercise these rights must be afforded to him throughout the interrogation. After such warnings have been given, and such opportunity afforded him, the individual may knowingly and intelligently waive these rights and agree to answer questions or make a statement. But unless and until such warnings and waiver are demonstrated by the prosecution at trial, no evidence obtained as a result of interrogation can be used against him.

* * * *

Decision

Reversed.

MYERS
v.
UNITED STATES.
272 U.S. 52, 47 S.Ct. 21, 71 L.Ed. 160
Reargued April 13, 14, 1925.
Decided Oct. 25, 1926.

Introduction

The presidential removal power case in which the Court held unconstitutional an 1876 law that required Senate consent before the president could dismiss a postmaster.

WESTLAW Summary

Suit by Lois P. Myers, administratrix of the estate of Frank S. Myers, against the United States. Judgment for defendant and plaintiff appeals. Affirmed.

Case Excerpts

Mr. Chief Justice TAFT delivered the opinion of the Court.

This case presents the question whether under the Constitution the President has the exclusive power of removing executive officers of the United States whom he has appointed by and with the advice and consent of the Senate.

Myers, appellant's intestate, was on July 21, 1917, appointed by the President, by and with the advice and consent of the Senate, to be a postmaster of the first class at Portland, Or., for a term of four years. On January 20, 1920, Myers' resignation was demanded. He refused the demand. On February 2, 1920, he was removed from office by order of the Postmaster General, acting by direction of the President. February 10th, Myers sent a petition to the President and another to the Senate committee on post offices, asking to be heard, if any charges were filed. He protested to the department against his removal, and continued to do so until the end of his term. He pursued no other occupation and drew compensation for no other service during the interval. On April 21, 1921, he brought this suit in the Court of Claims for his salary from the date of his removal, which, as claimed by supplemental petition filed after July 21, 1921, the end of his term, amounted to $8,838.71. In August, 1920, the President made a recess appointment of one Jones, who took office September 19, 1920.

The Court of Claims gave judgment against Myers and this is an appeal from that judgment. The court held that he had lost his right of action because of his delay in suing * * *. [The case law suggests] that when a United States officer is dismissed, whether in disregard of the law or from mistake as to the facts of his case, he must promptly take effective action to assert his rights. But we do not find that Myers failed in this regard. He was constant in his efforts at reinstatement. A hearing before the Senate committee could not be had till the notice of his removal was sent to the Senate or his successor was nominated. From the time of his removal until the end of his term, there were three sessions of the Senate without such notice or nomination. He put off bringing his suit until the expiration of the Sixty-Sixth Congress, March 4, 1921. After that, and three months before his term expired, he filed his petition. Under these circumstances, we think his suit was not too late. Indeed the Solicitor General, while not formally confessing error in this respect, conceded at the bar that no laches had been shown.

* * * *

The Senate did not consent to the President's removal of Myers during his term. If [the applicable] statute in its requirement that his term should be four years unless sooner removed by the President by and with the consent of the Senate is valid, the appellant, Myers' administratrix, is entitled to recover his unpaid salary for his full term and the judgment of the Court of Claims must be reversed. The government maintains that the requirement is invalid, for the reason that under article 2 of the Constitution the President's power of removal of executive officers appointed by him with the advice and consent of the Senate is full and complete without consent of the Senate. If this view is sound, the removal of Myers by the President without the Senate's consent was legal, and the judgment of the Court of Claims against the appellant was correct, and must be affirmed, though for a different reason from the given by that court. We are therefore confronted by the constitutional question and cannot avoid it.

* * * *

The question where the power of removal of executive officers appointed by the President by and with the advice and consent of the Senate was vested, was presented early in the first session of the First Congress. There is no express provision respecting removals in the Constitution, except as section 4 of article 2 provides for removal from office by impeachment. * * *

* * * *

The requirement of the second section of article 2 that the Senate should advise and consent to the presidential appointments, was to be strictly construed. The words of section 2, following the general grant of executive power under section 1, were either an enumeration and emphasis of specific functions of the executive, not all inclusive, or were limitations upon the general grant of the executive power, and as such, being limitations, should not be enlarged beyond the words used. The executive power was given in general terms strengthened by specific terms where emphasis was regarded as appropriate, and was limited by direct expressions where limitation was needed, and the fact that no express limit was placed on the power of removal by the executive was convincing indication that none was intended.

* * * *

The history of the clause by which the Senate was given a check upon the President's power of appointment makes it clear that it was not prompted by any desire to limit removals. As already pointed out, the important purpose of those who brought about the restriction was to lodge in the Senate, where the small states had equal representation with the larger states, power to prevent the President from making too many appointments from the larger states. * * *

* * * *

We come now to consider an argument, advanced and strongly pressed on behalf of the complainant, that this case concerns only the removal of a postmaster, that a postmaster is an inferior officer, and that such an office was not included within the legislative decision of 1789, which related only to superior officers to be appointed by the President by and with the advice and consent of the Senate. This, it is said, is the distinction which Chief Justice Marshall had in mind in

Marbury v. Madison * * * in respect to the President's power of removal of a District of Columbia justice of the peace appointed and confirmed for a term of years. We find nothing in Marbury v. Madison to indicate any such distinction. * * *

The power to remove inferior executive officers, like that to remove superior executive officers, in an incident of the power to appoint them, and is in its nature an executive power. The authority of Congress given by the excepting clause to vest the appointment of such inferior officers in the heads of departments carries with it authority incidentally to invest the heads of departments with power to remove. It has been the practice of Congress to do so and this court has recognized that power. * * * But the court never has held, nor reasonably could hold, although it is argued to the contrary on behalf of the appellant, that the excepting clause enables Congress to draw to itself, or to either branch of it, the power to remove or the right to participate in the exercise of that power. To do this would be to go beyond the words and implications of that clause, and to infringe the constitutional principle of the separation of governmental powers.

Assuming, then, the power of Congress to regulate removals as incidental to the exercise of its constitutional power to vest appointments of inferior officers in the heads of departments, certainly so long as Congress does not exercise that power, the power of removal must remain where the Constitution places it, with the President, as part of the executive power, in accordance with the legislative decision of 1789 which we have been considering.

* * * *

It is said that for 40 years or more postmasters were all by law appointed by the Postmaster General. This was because Congress under the excepting clause so provided. But thereafter Congress required certain classes of them to be, as they now are, appointed by the President with the consent of the Senate. This is an indication that Congress deemed appointment by the President with the consent of the Senate essential to the public welfare, and until it is willing to vest their appointment in the head of the department they will be subject to removal by the President alone, and any legislation to the contrary must fall as in conflict with the Constitution.

Summing up, then, the facts as to acquiescence by all branches of the government in the legislative decision of 1789 as to executive officers, whether superior or inferior, we find that from 1789 until 1863, a period of 74 years, there was no act of Congress, no executive act, and no decision of this court at variance with the declaration of the First Congress; but there was, as we have seen, clear affirmative recognition of it by each branch of the government.

Our conclusion on the merits, sustained by the arguments before stated, is that article 2 grants to the President the executive power of the government-i.e., the general administrative control of those executing the laws, including the power of appointment and removal of executive officers-a conclusion confirmed by his obligation to take care that the laws be faithfully executed; that article 2 excludes the exercise of legislative power by Congress to provide for appointments and removals, except only as granted therein to Congress in the matter of inferior offices; that Congress is only given power to provide for appointments and removals of inferior officers after it has vested, and on condition that it does vest, their appointment in other authority than the President with the Senate's consent; that the provisions of the second section of article 2, which blend action by the legislative branch, or by part of it, in the work of the executive, are limitations to be strictly construed, and not to be extended by implication; that the President's power of removal is further established as an incident to his specifically enumerated function of appointment by and with the advice of the Senate, but that such incident does not by implication extend to removals the Senate's power of checking appointments; and, finally, that to hold otherwise would make it impossible for the President, in case of political or other difference with the Senate or Congress, to take care that the laws be faithfully executed.

Decision

Judgment affirmed.

NEW YORK TIMES Company
v.
UNITED STATES.
403 U.S. 713, 91 S.Ct. 2140, 29 L.Ed.2d 822
Argued June 26, 1971.
Decided June 30, 1971.

Introduction

A freedom of press/prior restraint case involving the publication of sensitive government documents relating to the government's policy in Vietnam from 1945 to 1967. The U.S. government attempted to suspend the publication of the so-called *Pentagon Papers*, but the Court held that the government could only prosecute after publication, not before.

WESTLAW Summary

The United States sought to enjoin newspapers from publishing contents of classified historical study on Viet Nam policy. In one case, the District Court for the Southern District of New York rendered judgment from which the Government appealed, and the Court of Appeals for the Second Circuit remanded and continued stay. In the other case, the District Court for the District of Columbia rendered judgment from which the Government appealed, and the Court of Appeals for the District of Columbia Circuit affirmed. In both cases certiorari was granted. The Supreme Court held that the Government had not met its burden of showing justification for the imposition of restraint on the publication of the contents of the study.

Case Excerpts

PER CURIAM.

We granted certiorari in these cases in which the United States seeks to enjoin the New York Times and the Washington Post from publishing the contents of a classified study entitled "History of U.S. Decision-Making Process on Viet Nam Policy.'

"Any system of prior restraints of expression comes to this Court bearing a heavy presumption against its constitutional validity.' (citations omitted) The Government "thus carries a heavy burden of showing justification for the imposition of such a restraint.' The District Court for the Southern District of New York in the New York Times case and the District Court for the District of Columbia and the Court of Appeals for the District of Columbia Circuit, in the Washington Post case held that the Government had not met that burden. We agree.

The judgment of the Court of Appeals for the District of Columbia Circuit is therefore affirmed. The order of the Court of Appeals for the Second Circuit is reversed and the case is remanded with directions to enter a judgment affirming the judgment of the District Court for the Southern District of New York. The stays entered June 25, 1971, by the Court are vacated. The judgments shall issue forthwith.

So ordered.

Mr. Justice BLACK, with whom Mr. Justice DOUGLAS joins, concurring.

I adhere to the view that the Government's case against the Washington Post should have been dismissed and that the injunction against the New York Times should have been vacated without oral argument when the cases were first presented to this Court. I believe that every moment's continuance of the injunctions against these newspapers amounts to a flagrant, indefensible, and continuing violation of the First Amendment. Furthermore, after oral argument, I agree completely that we must affirm the judgment of the Court of Appeals for the District of Columbia Circuit and reverse the judgment of the Court of Appeals for the Second Circuit * * *. In my view it is unfortunate that some of my Brethren are apparently willing to hold that the publication of news may sometimes be enjoined. Such a holding would make a shambles of the First Amendment.

Our Government was launched in 1789 with the adoption of the Constitution. The Bill of Rights, including the First Amendment, followed in 1791. Now, for the first time in the 182 years since the founding of the Republic, the federal courts are asked to hold that the

First Amendment does not mean what it says, but rather means that the Government can halt the publication of current news of vital importance to the people of this country.

In seeking injunctions against these newspapers and in its presentation to the Court, the Executive Branch seems to have forgotten the essential purpose and history of the First Amendment. When the Constitution was adopted, many people strongly opposed it because the document contained no Bill of Rights to safeguard certain basic freedoms. They especially feared that the new power s granted to a central government might be interpreted to permit the government to curtail freedom of religion, press, assembly, and speech. In response to an overwhelming public clamor, James Madison offered a series of amendments to satisfy citizens that these great liberties would remain safe and beyond the power of government to abridge. Madison proposed what later became the First Amendment in three parts, two of which are set out below, and one of which proclaimed: "The people shall not be deprived or abridged of their right to speak, to write, or to publish their sentiments; and the freedom of the press, as one of the great bulwarks of liberty, shall be inviolable.' The amendments were offered to curtail and restrict the general powers granted to the Executive, Legislative, and Judicial Branches two years before in the original Constitution. The Bill of Rights changed the original Constitution into a new charter under which no branch of government could abridge the people's freedoms of press, speech, religion, and assembly. Yet the Solicitor General argues and some members of the Court appear to agree that the general powers of the Government adopted in the original Constitution should be interpreted to limit and restrict the specific and emphatic guarantees of the Bill of Rights adopted later. I can imagine no greater perversion of history. Madison and the other Framers of the First Amendment, able men that they were, wrote in language they earnestly believed could never be misunderstood: "Congress shall make no law * * * abridging the freedom * * * of the press * * *.' Both the history and language of the First Amendment support the view that the press must be left free to publish news, whatever the source, without censorship, injunctions, or prior restraints.

In the First Amendment the Founding Fathers gave the free press the protection it must have to fulfill its essential role in our democracy.

The press was to serve the governed, not the governors. The Government's power to censor the press was abolished so that the press would remain forever free to censure the Government. The press was protected so that it could bare the secrets of government and inform the people. Only a free and unrestrained press can effectively expose deception in government. And paramount among the responsibilities of a free press is the duty to prevent any part of the government from deceiving the people and sending them off to distant lands to die of foreign fevers and foreign shot and shell. In my view, far from deserving condemnation for their courageous reporting, the New York Times, the Washington Post, and other newspapers should be commended for serving the purpose that the Founding Fathers saw so clearly. In revealing the workings of government that led to the Vietnam war, the newspapers nobly did precisely that which the Founders hoped and trusted they would do.

The Government's case here is based on premises entirely different from those that guided the Framers of the First Amendment. The Solicitor General has carefully and emphatically stated:

"Now, Mr. Justice (BLACK), your construction of * * * (the First Amendment) is well known, and I certainly respect it. You say that no law means no law, and that should be obvious. I can only say, Mr. Justice, that to me it is equally obvious that "no law' does not mean "no law', and I would seek to persuade the Court that that is true. * * * (T)here are other parts of the Constitution that grant powers and responsibilities to the Executive, and * * * the First Amendment was not intended to make it impossible for the Executive to function or to protect the security of the United States.'

And the Government argues in its brief that in spite of the First Amendment, "(t)he authority of the Executive Department to protect the nation against publication of information whose disclosure would endanger the national security stems from two interrelated sources: the constitutional power of the President over the conduct of foreign affairs and his authority as Commander-in-Chief.'

In other words, we are asked to hold that despite the First Amendment's emphatic command, the Executive Branch, the Congress, and the Judiciary can make laws enjoining publication of current news and abridging freedom of the press in the name of "national security.' The Government does not even attempt to rely on any act of Congress.

Instead it makes the bold and dangerously farreaching contention that the courts should take it upon themselves to "make' a law abridging freedom of the press in the name of equity, presidential power and national security, even when the representatives of the people in Congress have adhered to the command of the First Amendment and refused to make such a law. To find that the President has "inherent power' to halt the publication of news by resort to the courts would wipe out the First Amendment and destroy the fundamental liberty and security of the very people the Government hopes to make "secure.' No one can read the history of the adoption of the First Amendment without being convinced beyond any doubt that it was injunctions like those sought here that Madison and his collaborators intended to outlaw in this Nation for all time.

The word "security' is a broad, vague generality whose contours should not be invoked to abrogate the fundamental law embodied in the First Amendment. The guarding of military and diplomatic secrets at the expense of informed representative government provides no real security for our Republic. The Framers of the First Amendment, fully aware of both the need to defend a new nation and the abuses of the English and Colonial Governments, sought to give this new society strength and security by providing that freedom of speech, press, religion, and assembly should not be abridged. This thought was eloquently expressed in 1937 by Mr. Chief Justice Hughes-great man and great Chief Justice that he was-when the Court held a man could not be punished for attending a meeting run by Communists.

"The greater the importance of safeguarding the community from incitements to the overthrow of our institutions by force and violence, the more imperative is the need to preserve inviolate the constitutional rights of free speech, free press and free assembly in order to maintain the opportunity for free political discussion, to the end that government may be responsive to the will of the people and that changes, if desired, may be obtained by peaceful means. Therein lies the security of the Republic, the very foundation of constitutional government.'

Decision

Judgment of the Court of Appeals for the District of Columbia Circuit affirmed; order of the Court of Appeals for the Second Circuit reversed and case remanded with directions.

POWELL et al.
v.
State of **ALABAMA.**
287 U.S. 45, 53 S.Ct. 55, 77 L.Ed. 158
Argued Oct. 10, 1932.
Decided Nov. 7, 1932.

Introduction

A Sixth Amendment right to counsel case in which the Court ruled that the accused has a right to a lawyer in capital punishment cases.

WESTLAW Summary

Ozie Powell and two others, Haywood Patterson, and Charley Weems, were convicted of rape. The convictions were affirmed by the Supreme Court of Alabama and the defendants bring certiorari. The Supreme Court reversed the judgements and remanded the causes for further proceedings in accordance with the opinion.

Case Excerpts

Mr. Justice SUTHERLAND delivered the opinion of the Court.

These cases were argued together and submitted for decision as one case.

The petitioners, hereinafter referred to as defendants, are negroes charged with the crime of rape, committed upon the persons of two white girls. The crime is said to have been committed on March 25, 1931. The indictment was returned in a state court of first instance on March 31, and the record recites that on the same day the defendants were arraigned and entered pleas of not guilty. There is a further recital to the effect that upon the arraignment they were represented by counsel. But no counsel had been employed, and aside from a statement made by the trial judge several days later during a colloquy immediately preceding the trial, the record does not disclose when, or under what circumstances, an appointment of counsel was made, or who was appointed. During the colloquy referred to, the trial judge, in response to a question, said that he had appointed all the members of the bar for the purpose of arraigning the defendants and then of course anticipated that the members of the bar would continue to help the defendants if no counsel appeared. Upon the argument here both sides accepted that as a correct statement of the facts concerning the matter.

There was a severance upon the request of the state, and the defendants were tried in three several groups, as indicated above. As each of the three cases was called for trial, each defendant was arraigned, and, having the indictment read to him, entered a plea of not guilty. Whether the original arraignment and pleas were regarded as ineffective is not shown. Each of the three trials was completed within a single day. Under the Alabama statute the punishment for rape is to be fixed by the jury, and in its discretion may be from ten years imprisonment to death. The juries found defendants guilty and imposed the death penalty upon all. The trial court overruled motions for new trials and sentenced the defendants in accordance with the verdicts. The judgments were affirmed by the state supreme court. Chief Justice Anderson thought the defendants had not been accorded a fair trial and strongly dissented.

In this court the judgments are assailed upon the grounds that the defendants, and each of them, were denied due process of law and the equal protection of the laws, in contravention of the Fourteenth Amendment, specifically as follows: (1) They were not given a fair, impartial, and deliberate trial; (2) they were denied the right of counsel, with the accustomed incidents of consultation and opportunity of preparation for trial; and (3) they were tried before juries from which qualified members of their own race were systematically excluded. These questions were properly raised and saved in the courts below.

The only one of the assignments which we shall consider is the second, in respect of the denial of counsel; and it becomes unnecessary to discuss the facts of the case or the circumstances surrounding the prosecution except in so far as they reflect light upon that question.

The record shows that on the day when the offense is said to have been committed, these defendants, together with a number of other negroes, were upon a freight train on its way through Alabama. On the same train were seven white boys and the two white girls. A fight took place between the negroes and the white boys, in the course of which the white boys, with the exception of one named Gilley, were thrown off the train. A message was sent ahead, reporting the fight and asking that every negro be gotten off the train. The participants in the fight, and the two girls, were in an open gondola car. The two girls testified that each of them was assaulted by six different negroes in turn, and they identified the seven defendants as having been among the number. None of the white boys was called to testify, with the exception of Gilley, who was called in rebuttal.

Before the train reached Scottsboro, Ala., a sheriff's posse seized the defendants and two other negroes. Both girls and the negroes then were taken to Scottsboro, the county seat. Word of their coming and of the alleged assault had preceded them, and they were met at Scottsboro by a large crowd. It does not sufficiently appear that the defendants were seriously threatened with, or that they were actually in danger of, mob violence; but it does appear that the attitude of the community was one of great hostility. The sheriff thought it necessary to call for the militia to assist in safeguarding the prisoners. Chief Justice Anderson pointed out in his opinion that every step taken from the arrest and arraignment to the sentence was accompanied by the military. Soldiers took the defendants to Gadsden for safe-keeping, brought them back to Scottsboro for arraignment, returned them to Gadsden for safe-keeping while awaiting trial, escorted them to Scottsboro for trial a few days later, and guarded the courthouse and grounds at every stage of the proceedings. It is perfectly apparent that the proceedings, from beginning to end, took place in an atmosphere of tense, hostile, and excited public sentiment. During the entire time, the defendants were closely confined or were under military guard. The record does not disclose their ages, except that one of them was nineteen; but the record clearly indicates that most, if not all, of them were youthful, and they are constantly referred to as "the boys.' They were ignorant and illiterate. All of them were residents of other states, where alone members of their families or friends resided.

However guilty defendants, upon due inquiry, might prove to have been, they were, until convicted, presumed to be innocent. It was the duty of the court having their cases in charge to see that they were denied no necessary incident of a fair trial. With any error of the state court involving alleged contravention of the state statutes or Constitution we, of course, have nothing to do. The sole inquiry which we are permitted to make is whether the federal Constitution was contravened and as to that, we confine ourselves, as already suggested, to the inquiry whether the defendants were in substance denied the right of counsel, and if so, whether such denial infringes the due process clause of the Fourteenth Amendment.

* * * The record shows that immediately upon the return of the indictment defendants were arraigned and pleaded not guilty. Apparently they were not asked whether they had, or were able to employ, counsel, or wished to have counsel appointed; or whether they had friends or relatives who might assist in that regard if communicated with. * * *

It is hardly necessary to say that the right to counsel being conceded, a defendant should be afforded a fair opportunity to secure counsel of his own choice. Not only was that not done here, but such designation of counsel as was attempted was either so indefinite or so close upon the trial as to amount to a denial of effective and substantial aid in that regard. * * *

* * * *

It thus will be seen that until the very morning of the trial no lawyer had been named or definitely designated to represent the defendants. Prior to that time, the trial judge had "appointed all the members of the bar' for the limited "purpose of arraigning the defendants.' Whether they would represent the defendants thereafter, if no counsel appeared in their behalf, was a matter of speculation only, or, as the judge indicated, of mere anticipation on the part of the court. Such a designation, even if made for all purposes, would, in our opinion, have fallen far short of meeting, in any proper sense, a requirement for the appointment of counsel. How many lawyers were members of the bar does not appear; but, in the very nature of things, whether many or few, they would not, thus collectively named, have been given that clear appreciation of responsibility or impressed with that individual sense of duty which should and naturally would accompany the appointment of a selected member of the bar, specifically named and assigned.

* * * *

It is not enough to assume that counsel thus precipitated into the case thought there was no defense, and exercised their best judgment in proceeding to trial without preparation. Neither they nor the court could say what a prompt and thorough-going investigation might disclose as to the facts. No attempt was made to investigate. No opportunity to do so was given. Defendants were immediately hurried to trial. Chief Justice Anderson, after disclaiming any intention to criticize harshly counsel who attempted to represent defendants at the trials, said: "* * * The record indicates that the appearance was rather pro forma than zealous and active * * *.' Under the circumstances disclosed, we hold that defendants were not accorded the right of counsel in any substantial sense. * * *

* * * *

In the light of the facts outlined in the forepart of this opinion-the ignorance and illiteracy of the defendants, their youth, the circumstances of public hostility, the imprisonment and the close surveillance of the defendants by the military forces, the fact that their friends and families were all in other states and communication with them necessarily difficult, and above all that they stood in deadly peril of their lives-we think the failure of the trial court to give them reasonable time and opportunity to secure counsel was a clear denial of due process.

* * * *

The United States by statute and every state in the Union by express provision of law, or by the determination of its courts, make it the duty of the trial judge, where the accused is unable to employ counsel, to appoint counsel for him. In most states the rule applies broadly to all criminal prosecutions, in others it is limited to the more serious crimes, and in a very limited number, to capital cases. A rule adopted with such unanimous accord reflects, if it does not establish the inherent right to have counsel appointed at least in cases like the present, and lends convincing support to the conclusion we have reached as to the fundamental nature of that right.

The judgments must be reversed and the causes remanded for further proceedings not inconsistent with this opinion.

Decision

Judgments reversed.

Sally M. **REED**
v.
Cecil R. **REED**, Administrator, etc.
404 U.S. 71, 92 S.Ct. 251, 30 L.Ed.2d 225
Argued Oct. 19, 1971.
Decided Nov. 22, 1971.

Introduction

A civil rights/gender-classification case in which the Court ruled against an Idaho law that gave fathers preferences over mothers in taking care of their children's estates.

WESTLAW Summary

Proceedings on separate petitions by the mother and father of the decedent for administration of the decedent's estate. The Idaho Supreme Court reversed the order of the District Court of the Fourth Judicial District and reinstated the original order of the probate court which named the father administrator of the estate. The mother appealed. The Supreme Court held that an Idaho statute which provides that as between persons equally qualified to administer estates males must be preferred to females, is based solely on a discrimination prohibited by and is violative of the equal protection clause of the Fourteenth Amendment.

Case Excerpts

Mr. Chief Justice BURGER delivered the opinion of the Court.

Richard Lynn Reed, a minor, died intestate in Ada County, Idaho, on March 29, 1967. His adoptive parents, who had separated sometime prior to his death, are the parties to this appeal. Approximately seven months after Richard's death, his mother, appellant Sally Reed, filed a petition in the Probate Court of Ada County, seeking appointment as administratrix of her son's estate. Prior to the date set for a hearing on the mother's petition, appellee Cecil Reed, the father of the decedent, filed a competing petition seeking to have himself appointed administrator of the son's estate. The probate court held a joint hearing on the two petitions and thereafter ordered that letters of administration be issued to appellee Cecil Reed upon his taking the oath and filing the bond required by law. The court treated ss 15-312 and 15-314 of the Idaho Code as the controlling statutes and read those sections as compelling a preference for Cecil Reed because he was a male.

Section 15-312 designates the persons who are entitled to administer the estate of one who dies intestate. In making these designations, that section lists 11 classes of persons who are so entitled and provides, in substance, that the order in which those classes are listed in the section shall be determinative of the relative rights of competing applicants for letters of administration. One of the 11 classes so enumerated is "(t)he father or mother' of the person dying intestate. Under this section then appellant and appellee, being members of the same entitlement class, would seem to have been equally entitled to administer their son's estate. Section 15-314 provides, however, that [males must be preferred to females].

In issuing its order, the probate court implicitly recognized the equality of entitlement of the two applicants under s 15-312 and noted that neither of the applicants was under any legal disability; the court ruled, however, that appellee, being a male, was to be preferred to the female appellant "by reason of Section 15-314 of the Idaho Code.' In stating this conclusion, the probate judge gave no indication that he had attempted to determine the relative capabilities of the competing applicants to perform the functions incident to the administration of an estate. It seems clear the probate judge considered himself bound by statute to give preference to the male candidate over the female, each being otherwise "equally entitled.'

Sally Reed appealed from the probate court order, and her appeal was treated by the District Court of the Fourth Judicial District of Idaho as a constitutional attack on s 15-314. In dealing with the attack, that court held that the challenged section violated the Equal Protection Clause of the Fourteenth Amendment and was, therefore, void; the matter was ordered "returned to the Probate Court for its determination of which of the two parties' was better qualified to administer the estate.

This order was never carried out, however, for Cecil Reed took a further appeal to the Idaho Supreme Court, which reversed the District Court and reinstated the original order naming the father administrator of the estate. In reaching this result, the Idaho Supreme Court first dealt with the governing statutory law and held that under s 15-312 "a father and mother are "equally entitled' to letters of administration,' but the preference given to males by s 15-314 is "mandatory' and leaves no room for the exercise of a probate court's discretion in the appointment of administrators. Having thus definitively and authoritatively interpreted the statutory provisions involved, the Idaho Supreme Court then proceeded to examine, and reject, Sally Reed's contention that s 15-314 violates the Equal Protection Clause by giving a mandatory preference to males over females, without regard to their individual qualifications as potential estate administrators.

Sally Reed thereupon appealed for review by this Court * * *, and we noted probable jurisdiction. Having examined the record and considered the briefs and oral arguments of the parties, we have concluded that the arbitrary preference established in favor of males by s 15-314 of the Idaho Code cannot stand in the face of the Fourteenth Amendment's command that no State deny the equal protection of the laws to any person within its jurisdiction.

Idaho does not, of course, deny letters of administration to women altogether. Indeed, under s 15-312, a woman whose spouse dies intestate has a preference over a son, father, brother, or any other male relative of the decedent. Moreover, we can judicially notice that in this country, presumably due to the greater longevity of women, a large proportion of estates, both intestate and under wills of decedents, are administered by surviving widows.

Section 15-314 is restricted in its operation to those situations where competing applications for letters of administration have been filed by both male and female members of the same entitlement class established by s 15-312. In such situations, s 15-314 provides that different treatment be accorded to the applicants on the basis of their sex; it thus establishes a classification subject to scrutiny under the Equal Protection Clause.

In applying that clause, this Court has consistently recognized that the Fourteenth Amendment does not deny to States the power to treat different classes of persons in different ways. The Equal Protection Clause of that amendment does, however, deny to States the power to legislate that different treatment be accorded to persons placed by a statute into different classes on the basis of criteria wholly unrelated to the objective of that statute. A classification "must be reasonable, not arbitrary, and must rest upon some ground of difference having a fair and substantial relation to the object of the legislation, so that all persons similarly circumstanced shall be treated alike.' (citation omitted) The question presented by this case, then, is whether a difference in the sex of competing applicants for letters of administration bears a rational relationship to a state objective that is sought to be advanced by the operation of ss 15-312 and 15-314.

In upholding the latter section, the Idaho Supreme Court concluded that its objective was to eliminate one area of controversy when two or more persons, equally entitled under s 15-312, seek letters of administration and thereby present the probate court "with the issue of which one should be named.' The court also concluded that where such persons are not of the same sex, the elimination of females from consideration "is neither an illogical nor arbitrary method devised by the legislature to resolve an issue that would otherwise require a hearing as to the relative merits * * * of the two or more petitioning relatives * * *.' (citation omitted)

Clearly the objective of reducing the workload on probate courts by eliminating one class of contests is not without some legitimacy. The crucial question, however, is whether s 15-314 advances that objective in a manner consistent with the command of the Equal Protection Clause. We hold that it does not. To give a mandatory preference to members of either sex over members of the other, merely to accomplish the elimination of hearings on the merits, is to make the very kind of arbitrary legislative choice forbidden by the Equal Protection Clause of the Fourteenth Amendment; and whatever may be said as to the positive values of avoiding intrafamily controversy, the choice in this context may not lawfully be mandated solely on the basis of sex.

We note finally that if s 15-314 is viewed merely as a modifying appendage to s 15-312 and as aimed at the same objective, its constitutionality is not thereby saved. The objective of s 15-312 clearly is to establish degrees of entitlement of various classes of persons in accordance with their varying degrees and kinds of relationship to the intestate. Regardless of their sex, persons within any one of the enumerated classes of that secion are similarly situated with respect to that objective. By providing dissimilar treatment for men and women who are thus similarly situated, the challenged section violates the Equal Protection Clause.

The judgment of the Idaho Supreme Court is reversed and the case remanded for further proceedings not inconsistent with this opinion.

Decision

Reversed and remanded

REGENTS OF THE UNIVERSITY OF CALIFORNIA
v.
Allan **BAKKE.**
438 U.S. 265, 98 S.Ct. 2733, 57 L.Ed.2d 750
Argued Oct. 12, 1977.
Decided June 28, 1978.

Introduction

A civil rights/reverse discrimination case in which the Court allowed the University of California Davis Campus Medical School to admit students on the bases of race if the school's aim is to combat the effects of past discriminations. The Court held, nonetheless, that Bakke must be admitted to the medical school because its admissions policy had used race as the *sole* criterion for a limited number of "minority" positions.

WESTLAW Summary

A white male whose application to state medical school was rejected brought an action challenging the legality of the school's special admissions program under which 16 of the 100 positions in the class were reserved for "disadvantaged" minority students. The school cross-claimed for a declaratory judgment that its program was legal. The trial court declared the program illegal but refused to order the school to admit the applicant. The California Supreme Court affirmed the finding that the program was illegal and ordered the student admitted. The school sought certiorari. The Supreme Court held that: (1) the special admissions program was illegal, but (2) race may be one of a number of factors considered by the school in passing on applications, and (3) since the school could not show that the white applicant would not have been admitted even in the absence of the special admissions program, the applicant was entitled to be admitted.

Case Excerpts

Mr. Justice POWELL announced the judgment of the Court.

* * * *

The Medical School of the University of California at Davis opened in 1968 with an entering class of 50 students. In 1971, the size of the entering class was increased to 100 students, a level at which it remains. No admissions program for disadvantaged or minority students existed when the school opened, and the first class contained three Asians but no blacks, no Mexican-Americans, and no American Indians. Over the next two years, the faculty devised a special admissions program to increase the representation of "disadvantaged" students in each Medical School class. The special program consisted of a separate admissions system operating in coordination with the regular admissions process.

* * * *

From the year of the increase in class size-1971-through 1974, the special program resulted in the admission of 21 black students, 30 Mexican-Americans, and 12 Asians, for a total of 63 minority students. Over the same period, the regular admissions program produced 1 black, 6 Mexican-Americans, 276 and 37 Asians, for a total of 44 minority students. Although disadvantaged whites applied to the special program in large numbers, none received an offer of admission through that process. Indeed, in 1974, at least, the special committee explicitly considered only "disadvantaged" special applicants who were members of one of the designated minority groups.

Allan Bakke is a white male who applied to the Davis Medical School in 1973 under the general admissions program * * *. Despite a strong benchmark score of 468 out of 500, Bakke was rejected. His application had come late in the year, and no applicants in the general admissions process with scores below 470 were accepted after Bakke's application was completed. There were four special admissions slots unfilled at that time however, for which Bakke was not considered. * * *

Bakke's 1974 application was completed early in the year. His student interviewer gave him an overall rating of 94, finding him "friendly, well tempered, conscientious and delightful to speak with."

Id., His faculty interviewer was, by coincidence, the same Dr. Lowrey to whom he had written in protest of the special admissions program. * * * Dr. Lowrey gave Bakke the lowest of his six ratings, an 86; his total was 549 out of 600. Again, Bakke's application was rejected. In neither year did the chairman of the admissions committee, Dr. Lowrey, exercise his discretion to place Bakke on the waiting list. In both years, applicants were admitted under the special program with grade point averages, MCAT scores, and benchmark scores significantly lower than Bakke's.

After the second rejection, Bakke filed the instant suit in the Superior Court of California. He sought mandatory, injunctive, and declaratory relief compelling his admission to the Medical School. * * * The University cross-complained for a declaration that its special admissions program was lawful. The trial court found that the special program operated as a racial quota, because minority applicants in the special program were rated only against one another. Declaring that the University could not take race into account in making admissions decisions, the trial court held the challenged program violative of the Federal Constitution, the State Constitution, and Title VI. The court refused to order Bakke's admission, however, holding that he had failed to carry his burden of proving that he would have been admitted but for the existence of the special program.

Bakke appealed from the portion of the trial court judgment denying him admission, and the University appealed from the decision that its special admissions program was unlawful and the order enjoining it from considering race in the processing of applications. The Supreme Court of California transferred the case directly from the trial court, "because of the importance of the issues involved." The California court accepted the findings of the trial court with respect to the University's program. Because the special admissions program involved a racial classification, the Supreme Court held itself bound to apply strict scrutiny. It then turned to the goals the University presented as justifying the special program. * * * Without passing on the state constitutional or the federal statutory grounds cited in the trial court's judgment, the California court held that the Equal Protection Clause of the Fourteenth Amendment required that "no applicant may be rejected because of his race, in favor of another who is less qualified, as measured by standards applied without regard to race." (citation omitted)

* * * *

In this Court the parties neither briefed nor argued the applicability of Title VI of the Civil Rights Act of 1964. Rather, as had the California court, they focused exclusively upon the validity of the special admissions program under the Equal Protection Clause. * * *

* * * *

En route to this crucial battle over the scope of judicial review, the parties fight a sharp preliminary action over the proper characterization of the special admissions program. Petitioner prefers to view it as establishing a "goal" of minority representation in the Medical School. Respondent, echoing the courts below, labels it a racial quota.

This semantic distinction is beside the point: The special admissions program is undeniably a classification based on race and ethnic background. To the extent that there existed a pool of at least minimally qualified minority applicants to fill the 16 special admissions seats, white applicants could compete only for 84 seats in the entering class, rather than the 100 open to minority applicants. Whether this limitation is described as a quota or a goal, it is a line drawn on the basis of race and ethnic status.

The guarantees of the Fourteenth Amendment extend to all persons. Its language is explicit: "No State shall ... deny to any person within its jurisdiction the equal protection of the laws." It is settled beyond question that the "rights created by the first section of the Fourteenth Amendment are, by its terms, guaranteed to the individual. The rights established are personal rights." (citations omitted) The guarantee of equal protection cannot mean one thing when applied to one individual and something else when applied to a person of another color. If both are not accorded the same protection, then it is not equal.

* * * *

Petitioner urges us to adopt for the first time a more restrictive view of the Equal Protection Clause and hold that discrimination against members of the white "majority" cannot be suspect if its purpose can be characterized as "benign." The clock of our liberties, however, cannot be turned back to 1868. * * * "The Fourteenth Amendment is not directed solely against discrimination due to a "two-class theory'-that is, based upon differences between "white' and Negro." (citation omitted)

Once the artificial line of a "two-class theory" of the Fourteenth Amendment is put aside, the difficulties entailed in varying the level of judicial review according to a perceived "preferred" status of a particular racial or ethnic minority are intractable. The concepts of "majority" and "minority" necessarily reflect temporary arrangements and political judgments. As observed above, the white "majority" itself is composed of various minority groups, most of which can lay claim to a history of prior discrimination at the hands of the State and private individuals. Not all of these groups can receive preferential treatment and corresponding judicial tolerance o f distinctions drawn in terms of race and nationality, for then the only "majority" left would be a new minority of white Anglo-Saxon Protestants. There is no principled basis for deciding which groups would merit "heightened judicial solicitude" and which would not. * * *

* * * *

In summary, it is evident that the Davis special admissions program involves the use of an explicit racial classification never before countenanced by this Court. It tells applicants who are not Negro, Asian, or Chicano that they are totally excluded from a specific percentage of the seats in an entering class. No matter how strong their qualifications, quantitative and extracurricular, including their own potential for contribution to educational diversity, they are never afforded the chance to compete with applicants from the preferred groups for the special admissions seats. At the same time, the preferred applicants have the opportunity to compete for every seat in the class.

In enjoining petitioner from ever considering the race of any applicant, however, the courts below failed to recognize that the State has a substantial interest that legitimately may be served by a properly devised admissions program involving the competitive consideration of race and ethnic origin. For this reason, so much of the California court's judgment as enjoins petitioner from any consideration of the race of any applicant must be reversed.

With respect to respondent's entitlement to an injunction directing his admission to the Medical School, petitioner has conceded that it could not carry its burden of proving that, but for the existence of its unlawful special admissions program, respondent still would not have been admitted. Hence, respondent is entitled to the injunction, and that portion of the judgment must be affirmed.

Decision

Affirmed in part and reversed in part.

B. A. **REYNOLDS**, et al.,
v.
M. O. **SIMS** et al.
377 U.S. 533, 84 S.Ct. 1362, 12 L.Ed.2d 506
Argued Nov. 13, 1963.
Decided June 15, 1964.
Rehearing Denied Oct. 12, 1964.

Introduction

A Congressional reapportionment case in which the Court ruled that both chambers of a state legislature must be apportioned with equal populations in each district. This "one-person, one-vote" principle had already been applied to Congressional districts in *Wesberry v. Sanders.*

WESTLAW Summary

Alabama legislative apportionment cases. The three-judge United States District Court for the Middle District of Alabama issued its decision, and appeals were taken. The Supreme Court held that the existing and two legislatively proposed plans for the apportionment of seats in the two houses of the Alabama Legislature were invalid under the Equal Protection Clause because the apportionment was not based on population and was completely lacking in rationality.

Case Excerpts

Mr. Chief Justice WARREN delivered the opinion of the Court.

Involved in these cases are an appeal and two cross-appeals from a decision of the Federal District Court for the Middle District of Alabama holding invalid, under the Equal Protection Clause of the Federal Constitution, the existing and two legislative proposed plans for the apportionment of seats in the two houses of the Alabama Legislature, and ordering into effect a temporary reapportionment plan comprised of parts of the proposed but judicially disapproved measures.

On August 26, 1961, the original plaintiffs, residents, taxpayers and voters of Jefferson County, Alabama, filed a complaint in the United States District Court for the Middle District of Alabama, in their own behalf and on behalf of all similarly situated Alabama voters, challenging the apportionment of the Alabama Legislature. * * * The complaint alleged a deprivation of rights under the Alabama Constitution and under the Equal Protection Clause of the Fourteenth Amendment, and asserted that the District Court had jurisdiction under provisions of the Civil Rights Act.

* * * *

Plaintiffs below alleged that the last apportionment of the Alabama Legislature was based on the 1900 federal census, despite the requirement of the State Constitution that the legislature be reapportioned decennially. They asserted that, since the population growth in the State from 1900 to 1960 had been uneven, Jefferson and other counties were now victims of serious discrimination with respect to the allocation of legislative representation. As a result of the failure of the legislature to reapportion itself, plaintiffs asserted, they were denied "equal suffrage in free and equal elections * * * and the equal protection of the laws' in violation of the Alabama Constitution and the Fourteenth Amendment to the Federal Constitution. * * *

* * * Under the existing provisions, applying 1960 census figures, only 25.1% of the State's totel population resided in districts represented by a majority of the members of the Senate, and only 25.7% lived in counties which could elect a majority of the members of the House of Representatives. Population-variance ratios of up to about 41-to-1 existed in the Senate, and up to about 16-to-1 in the House. Bullock County, with a population of only 13,462, and Henry County, with a population of only 15,286, each were allocated two seats in the Alabama House, whereas Mobile County, with a population of 314,301, was given only three seats, and Jefferson County, with 634,864 people, had only seven representatives. With respect to senatorial apportionment, since the pertinent Alabama constitutional provisions had been consistently construed as prohibiting the giving of more than one Senate seat to any one county, Jefferson County, with over 600,000 people, was given only one senator, as was Lowndes County, with a

1960 population of only 15,417, and Wilcox County, with only 18,739 people.

* * * *

Undeniably the Constitution of the United States protects the right of all qualified citizens to vote, in state as well as in federal elections. A consistent line of decisions by this Court in cases involving attempts to deny or restrict the right of suffrage has made this indelibly clear. It has been repeatedly recognized that all qualified voters have a constitutionally protected right to vote * * *.

* * * *

A predominant consideration in determining whether a State's legislative apportionment scheme constitutes an invidious discrimination violative of rights asserted under the Equal Protection Clause is that the rights allegedly impaired are individual and personal in nature. * * * While the result of a court decision in a state legislative apportionment controversy may be to require the restructuring of the geographical distribution of seats in a state legislature, the judicial focus must be concentrated upon ascertaining whether there has been any discrimination against certain of the State's citizens which constitutes an impermissible impairment of their constitutionally protected right to vote. * * * Especially since the right to exercise the franchise in a free and unimpaired manner is preservative of other basic civil and political rights, any alleged infringement of the right of citizens to vote must be carefully and meticulously scrutinized. * * *

Legislators represent people, not trees or acres. Legislators are elected by voters, not farms or cities or economic interests. As long as ours is a representative form of government, and our legislatures are those instruments of government elected directly by and directly representative of the people, the right to elect legislators in a free and unimpaired fashion is a bedrock of our political system. It could hardly be gainsaid that a constitutional claim had been asserted by an allegation that certain otherwise qualified voters had been entirely prohibited from voting for members of their state legislature. And, if a State should provide that the votes of citizens i n one part of the State should be given two times, or five times, or 10 times the weight of votes of citizens in another part of the State, it could hardly be contended that the right to vote of those residing in the disfavored areas had not been effectively diluted. It would appear extraordinary to suggest that a State could be constitutionally permitted to enact a law providing that certain of the State's voters could vote two, five, or 10 times for their legislative representatives, while voters living elsewhere could vote only once. And it is inconceivable that a state law to the effect that, in counting votes for legislators, the votes of citizens in one part of the State would be multiplied by two, five, or 10, while the votes of persons in another area would be counted only at face value, could be constitutionally sustainable. Of course, the effect of state legislative districting schemes which give the same number of representatives to unequal numbers of constituents is identical. * * *

Logically, in a society ostensibly grounded on representative government, it would seem reasonable that a majority of the people of a State could elect a majority of that State's legislators. To conclude differently, and to sanction minority control of state legislative bodies, would appear to deny majority rights in a way that far surpasses any possible denial of minority rights that might otherwise be thought to result. Since legislatures are responsible for enacting laws by which all citizens are to be governed, they should be bodies which are collectively responsive to the popular will. And the concept of equal protection has been traditionally viewed as requiring the uniform treatment of persons standing in the same relation to the governmental action questioned or challenged. With respect to the allocation of legislative representation, all voters, as citizens of a State, stand in the same relation regardless of where they live. * * *

* * * *

We hold that, as a basic constitutional standard, the Equal Protection Clause requires that the seats in both houses of a bicameral state legislature must be apportioned on a population basis. Simply stated, an individual's right to vote for state legislators is unconstitutionally impaired when its weight is in a substantial fashion diluted when compared with votes of citizens living on other parts of the State. * * *

* * * *

Since we find the so-called federal analogy inapposite to a consideration of the constitutional validity of state legislative apportionment schemes, we necessarily hold that the Equal Protection Clause requires both houses of a state legislature to be apportioned on a population basis. The right of a citizen to equal representation and to have his vote weighted equally with those of all other citizens in the election of members of one house of a bicameral state legislature would amount to little if States could effectively submerge the equal-population principle in the apportionment of seats in the other house. * * * In summary, we can perceive no constitutional difference, with respect to the geographical distribution of state legislative representation, between the two houses of a bicameral state legislature.

* * * *

We find, therefore, that the action taken by the District Court in this case, in ordering into effect a reapportionment of both houses of the Alabama Legislature for purposes of the 1962 primary and general elections, by using the best parts of the two proposed plans which it had found, as a whole, to be invalid, was an appropriate and well-considered exercise of judicial power. Admittedly, the lower court's ordered plan was intended only as a temporary and provisional measure and the District Court correctly indicated that the plan was invalid as a permanent apportionment. In retaining jurisdiction while deferring a hearing on the issuance of a final injunction in order to give the provisionally reapportioned legislature an opportunity to act effectively, the court below proceeded in a proper fashion. Since the District Court evinced its realization that its ordered reapportionment could not be sustained as the basis for conducting the 1966 election of Alabama legislators, and avowedly intends to take some further action should the reapportioned Alabama Legislature fail to enact a constitutionally valid, permanent apportionment scheme in the interim, we affirm the judgment below and remand the cases for further proceedings consistent with the views stated in this opinion. It is so ordered.

Decision

Affirmed and remanded.

ROCHIN
v.
People of **CALIFORNIA.**
342 U.S. 165, 72 S.Ct. 205, 96 L.Ed. 183
Argued Oct. 16, 1951.
Decided Jan. 2, 1952.

Introduction

A due process of law/procedural due process case, sometimes referred to as "the stomach pumping case" in which a suspected illegal drug user was taken to a hospital and administered a liquid that forced him to vomit. Morphine capsules thereby recovered were used to convict him of violating the state's narcotics laws. The Court overruled the conviction holding that it violated the Fourteenth Amendment's guarantee of procedural due process.

WESTLAW Summary

Antonio Richard Rochin was convicted in the Superior Court of Los Angeles County of possessing a preparation of morphine in violation of the state health and safety code and he appealed. The District Court of Appeal for the Second Appellate District of the State of California affirmed the conviction. The Supreme Court of California denied without opinion the defendant's petition for a hearing, and the defendant brought certiorari. The Supreme Court held that, where deputy sheriffs having some information that the accused was selling narcotics, entered the open door of the dwelling house and forced open the door to the accused's bedroom and forcibly attempted to extract capsules which the accused swallowed, and at a hospital a physician, at deputy sheriffs' direction, forced an emetic solution through a tube into the accused's stomach against his will, and this "stomach pumping' produced vomiting, and in the vom ited matter were found two capsules containing morphine, the use of the capsules in California court to obtain the conviction of the defendant for illegal possession of morphine violated the Due Process Clause of Fourteenth Amendment.

Case Excerpts

Mr. Justice FRANKFURTER delivered the opinion of the Court.

Having "some information that (the petitioner here) was selling narcotics,' three deputy sheriffs of the County of Los Angeles, on the morning of July 1, 1949, made for the two-story dwelling house in which Rochin lived with his mother, common-law wife, brothers and sisters. Finding the outside door open, they entered and then forced open the door to Rochin's room on the second floor. Inside they found petitioner sitting partly dressed on the side of the bed, upon which his wife was lying. On a "night stand' beside the bed the deputies spied two capsules. When asked "Whose stuff is this?' Rochin seized the capsules and put them in his mouth. A struggle ensued, in the course of which the three officers "jumped upon him' and attempted to extract the capsules. The force they applied proved unavailing against Rochin's resistance. He was handcuffed and taken to a hospital. At the direction of one of the officers a doctor forced an emetic solution through a tube into Rochin's stomach against his will. This "stomach pumping' produced vomiting. In the vomited matter were found two capsules which proved to contain morphine.

Rochin was brought to trial before a California Superior Court, sitting without a jury, on the charge of possessing "a preparation of morphine' in violation of the California Health and Safety Code 1947, s 11500. Rochin was convicted and sentenced to sixty days' imprisonment. The chief evidence against him was the two capsules. They were admitted over petitioner's objection, although the means of obtaining them was frankly set forth in the testimony by one of the deputies, substantially as here narrated.

On appeal, the District Court of Appeal affirmed the conviction, despite the finding that the officer "were guilty of unlawfully breaking into and entering defendant's room and were guilty of unlawfully assaulting and battering defendant while in the room', and "were guilty of unlawfully assaulting, battering, torturing and falsely imprisoning the defendant at the alleged hospital.' (citation omitted) * * *

This Court granted certiorari because a serious question is raised as to the limitations which the Due Process Clause of the Fourteenth

Amendment imposes on the conduct of criminal proceedings by the States.

* * * *

[We] are compelled to conclude that the proceedings by which this conviction was obtained do more than offend some fastidious squeamishness or private sentimentalism about combatting crime too energetically. This is conduct that shocks the conscience. Illegally breaking into the privacy of the petitioner, the struggle to open his mouth and remove what was there, the forcible extraction of his stomach's contents-this course of proceeding by agents of government to obtain evidence is bound to offend even hardened sensibilities. They are methods too close to the rack and the screw to permit of constitutional differentiation.

It has long since ceased to be true that due process of law is heedless of the means by which otherwise relevant and credible evidence is obtained. This was not true even before the series of recent cases enforced the constitutional principle that the States may not base convictions upon confessions, however much verified, obtained by coercion. These decisions are not arbitrary exceptions to the comprehensive right of States to fashion their own rules of evidence for criminal trials. They are not sports in our constitutional law but applications of a general principle. They are only instances of the general requirement that States in their prosecutions respect certain decencies of civilized conduct. Due process of law, as a historic and generative principle, precludes defining, and thereby confining, these standards of conduct more precisely than to say that convictions cannot be brought about by methods that offend "a sense of justice.' (citation omitted) It would be a stultification of the responsibility which the course of constitutional history has cast upon this Court to hold that in order to convict a man the police cannot extract by force what is in his mind but can extract what is in his stomach.

To attempt in this case to distinguish what lawyers call "real evidence' from verbal evidence is to ignore the reasons for excluding coerced confessions. Use of involuntary verbal confessions in State criminal trials is constitutionally obnoxious not only because of their unreliability. They are inadmissible under the Due Process Clause even though statements contained in them may be independently established as true. Coerced confessions offend the community's sense of fair play and decency. So here, to sanction the brutal conduct which naturally enough was condemned by the court whose judgment is before us, would be to afford brutality the cloak of law. Nothing would be more calculated to discredit law and thereby to brutalize the temper of a society.

In deciding this case we do not heedlessly bring into question decisions in many States dealing with essentially different, even if related, problems. We therefore put to one side cases which have arisen in the State courts through use of modern methods and devices for discovering wrongdoers and bringing them to book. It does not fairly represent these decisions to suggest that they legalize force so brutal and so offensive to human dignity in securing evidence from a suspect as is revealed by this record. Indeed the California Supreme Court has not sanctioned this mode of securing a conviction. It merely exercised its discretion to decline a review of the conviction. All the California judges who have expressed themselves in this case have condemned the conduct in the strongest language.

We are not unmindful that hypothetical situations can be conjured up, standing imperceptibly from the circumstances of this case and by gradations producing practical differences despite seemingly logical extensions. But the Constitution is "intended to preserve practical and substantial rights, not to maintain theories.' (citation omitted)

On the facts of this case the conviction of the petitioner has been obtained by methods that offend the Due Process Clause. The judgment below must be reversed.

Decision

Reversed.

Jane **ROE**, et al.
v.
Henry **WADE**.
410 U.S. 113, 93 S.Ct. 705, 35 L.Ed.2d 147
Argued Dec. 13, 1971.
Reargued Oct. 11, 1972.
Decided Jan. 22, 1973.
Rehearing Denied Feb. 26, 1973.

Introduction

A privacy case in which the Court ruled that state anti-abortion laws were unconstitutional except when they applied to the last three months of pregnancy.

WESTLAW Summary

Action was brought for declaratory and injunctive relief respecting Texas criminal abortion laws which were claimed to be unconstitutional. A three-judge United States District Court for the Northern District of Texas entered judgment declaring the laws to be unconstitutional and an appeal was taken. The Supreme Court held that the Texas criminal abortion statutes prohibiting abortions at any stage of a pregnancy except to save the life of the mother are unconstitutional; that prior to approximately the end of the first trimester the abortion decision and its effectuation must be left to the medical judgment of the pregnant woman's attending physician, subsequent to approximately the end of the first trimester the state may regulate the abortion procedure in ways reasonably related to maternal health, and at the stage subsequent to viability the state may regulate and even proscribe abortion except where necessary in appropriate medical judgment for the preservation of the life or health of the mother.

Case Excerpts

Mr. Justice BLACKMUN delivered the opinion of the Court.

This Texas federal appeal and its Georgia companion, Doe v. Bolton, present constitutional challenges to state criminal abortion legislation. The Texas statutes under attack here are typical of those that have been in effect in many States for approximately a century. The Georgia statutes, in contrast, have a modern cast and are a legislative product that, to an extent at least, obviously reflects the influences of recent attitudinal changes, of advancing medical knowledge and techniques, and of new thinking about an old issue.

* * * *

The Texas statutes that concern us here are Arts. 1191-1194 and 1196 of the State's Penal Code. These make it a crime to "procure an abortion,' as therein defined, or to attempt one, except with respect to "an abortion procured or attempted by medical advice for the purpose of saving the life of the mother.' Similar statutes are in existence in a majority of the States. * * *

Jane Roe, a single woman who was residing in Dallas County, Texas, instituted this federal action in March 1970 against the District Attorney of the county. She sought a declaratory judgment that the Texas criminal abortion statutes were unconstitutional on their face, and an injunction restraining the defendant from enforcing the statutes.

Roe alleged that she was unmarried and pregnant; that she wished to terminate her pregnancy by an abortion "performed by a competent, licensed physician, under safe, clinical conditions'; that she was unable to get a "legal' abortion in Texas because her life did not appear to be threatened by the continuation of her pregnancy; and that she could not afford to travel to another jurisdiction in order to secure a legal abortion under safe conditions. She claimed that the Texas statutes were unconstitutionally vague and that they abridged her right of personal privacy, protected by the First, Fourth, Fifth, Ninth, and Fourteenth Amendments. By an amendment to her complaint Roe purported to sue "on behalf of herself and all other women' similarly situated.

* * * *

Viewing Roe's case as of the time of its filing and thereafter until as late as May, there can be little dispute that it then presented a case or controversy and that, wholly apart from the class aspects, she, as a pregnant single woman thwarted by the Texas criminal abortion laws, had standing to challenge those statutes. * * *

* * * *

The usual rule in federal cases is that an actual controversy must exist at stages of appellate or certiorari review, and not simply at the date the action is initiated. * * *

But when, as here, pregnancy is a significant fact in the litigation, the normal 266-day human gestation period is so short that the pregnancy will come to term before the usual appellate process is complete. If that termination makes a case moot, pregnancy litigation seldom will survive much beyond the trial stage, and appellate review will be effectively denied. Our law should not be that rigid. Pregnancy often comes more than once to the same woman, and in the general population, if man is to survive, it will always be with us. Pregnancy provides a classic justification for a conclusion of nonmootness. It truly could be "capable of repetition, yet evading review.' (citation omitted)

We, therefore, agree with the District Court that Jane Roe had standing to undertake this litigation, that she presented a justiciable controversy, and that the termination of her 1970 pregnancy has not rendered her case moot.

* * * *

The principal thrust of appellant's attack on the Texas statutes is that they improperly invade a right, said to be possessed by the pregnant woman, to choose to terminate her pregnancy. Appellant would discover this right in the concept of personal "liberty' embodied in the Fourteenth Amendment's Due Process Clause; or in personal marital, familial, and sexual privacy said to be protected by the Bill of Rights * * *.

* * * *

It has been argued occasionally that these laws were the product of a Victorian social concern to discourage illicit sexual conduct. * * *

A second reason is concerned with abortion as a medical procedure. When most criminal abortion laws were first enacted, the procedure was a hazardous one for the woman. * * *

* * * Mortality rates for women undergoing early abortions, where the procedure is legal, appear to be as low as or lower than the rates for normal childbirth. Consequently, any interest of the State in protecting the woman from an inherently hazardous procedure, except

when it would be equally dangerous for her to forgo it, has largely disappeared. * * *

The third reason is the State's interest-some phrase it in terms of duty-in protecting prenatal life. Some of the argument for this justification rests on the theory that a new human life is present from the moment of conception. * * *

The Constitution does not explicitly mention any right of privacy. In a line of decisions, however, the Court has recognized that a right of personal privacy, or a guarantee of certain areas or zones of privacy, does exist under the Constitution. * * *

This right of privacy, whether it be founded in the Fourteenth Amendment's concept of personal liberty and restrictions upon state action, as we feel it is, or, as the District Court determined, in the Ninth Amendment's reservation of rights to the people, is broad enough to encompass a woman's decision whether or not to terminate her pregnancy. The detriment that the State would impose upon the pregnant woman by denying this choice altogether is apparent. Specific and direct harm medically diagnosable even in early pregnancy may be involved. Maternity, or additional offspring, may force upon the woman a distressful life and future. Psychological harm may be imminent. Mental and physical health may be taxed by child care. There is also the distress, for all concerned, associated with the unwanted child, and there is the problem of bringing a child into a family already unable, psychologically and otherwise, to care for it. In other cases, as in this one, the additional difficulties and continuing stigma of unwed motherhood may be involved. All these are factors the woman and her responsible physician necessarily will consider in consultation.

On the basis of elements such as these, appellant and some amici argue that the woman's right is absolute and that she is entitled to terminate her pregnancy at whatever time, in whatever way, and for whatever reason she alone chooses. With this we do not agree. Appellant's arguments that Texas either has no valid interest at all in regulating the abortion decision, or no interest strong enough to support any limitation upon the woman's sole determination, are unpersuasive. The Court's decisions recognizing a right of privacy also acknowledge that some state regulation in areas protected by that right is appropriate. As noted above, a State may properly assert important interests in safeguarding health, in maintaining medical standards, and in protecting potential life. At some point in pregnancy, these respective interests become sufficiently compelling to sustain regulation of the factors that govern the abortion decision. The privacy right involved, therefore, cannot be said to be absolute. In fact, it is not clear to us that the claim asserted by some amici that one has an unlimited right to do with one's body as one pleases bears a close relationship to the right of privacy previously articulated in the Court's decisions. * * *

We, therefore, conclude that the right of personal privacy includes the abortion decision, but that this right is not unqualified and must be considered against important state interests in regulation.

* * * *

* * * We repeat, however, that the State does have an important and legitimate interest in preserving and protecting the health of the pregnant woman, whether she be a resident of the State or a nonresident who seeks medical consultation and treatment there, and that it has still another important and legitimate interest in protecting the potentiality of human life. These interests are separate and distinct. Each grows in substantiality as the woman approaches term and, at a point during pregnancy, each becomes "compelling.'

With respect to the State's important and legitimate interest in the health of the mother, the "compelling' point, in the light of present medical knowledge, is at approximately the end of the first trimester. This is so because of the now-established medical fact that until the end of the first trimester mortality in abortion may be less than mortality in normal childbirth. It follows that, from and after this point, a State may regulate the abortion procedure to the extent that the regulation reasonably relates to the preservation and protection of maternal health. * * *

This means, on the other hand, that, for the period of pregnancy prior to this "compelling' point, the attending physician, in consultation with his patient, is free to determine, without regulation by the State, that, in his medical judgment, the patient's pregnancy should be terminated. If that decision is reached, the judgment may be effectuated by an abortion free of interference by the State.

With respect to the State's important and legitimate interest in potential life, the "compelling' point is at viability. This is so because the fetus then presumably has the capability of meaningful life outside the mother's womb. State regulation protective of fetal life after viability thus has both logical and biological justifications. If the State is interested in protecting fetal life after viability, it may go so far as to proscribe abortion during that period, except when it is necessary to preserve the life or health of the mother.

Measured against these standards, Art. 1196 of the Texas Penal Code, in restricting legal abortions to those "procured or attempted by medical advice for the purpose of saving the life of the mother,' sweeps too broadly. The statute makes no distinction between abortions performed early in pregnancy and those performed later, and it limits to a single reason, "saving' the mother's life, the legal justification for the procedure. The statute, therefore, cannot survive the constitutional attack made upon it here.

*   *   *   *

Decision

Affirmed in part and reversed in part.

SMITH
v.
ALLWRIGHT,
321 U.S. 649, 64 S.Ct. 657, 88 L.Ed. 987
Reargued Jan. 12, 1944.
Decided April 3, 1944.
As Amended June 12, 1944.
Rehearing Denied May 8, 1944.

Introduction

A voting rights case in which the Court declared that the white primary was a violation of the Fifteenth Amendment. The Court reasoned that the political party was actually performing a state function and holding a primary election and therefore not acting as a private group.

WESTLAW Summary

Action by Lonnie E. Smith against S. E. Allwright, Election Judge, and James E. Liuzza, Associate Election Judge, Forty-Eighth Precinct of Harris County, Texas, for a declaratory judgment, and for damages due to the refusal of the defendants to permit the plaintiff to cast a ballot in a primary election for nomination of Democratic candidates for the United States Senate and House of Representatives, and Governor and other state officers. A judgment dismissing the petition was affirmed by the Circuit Court of Appeals. The Supreme Court granted certiorari and reversed.

Case Excerpts

Mr. Justice REED delivered the opinion of the Court.

This writ of certiorari brings here for review a claim for damages in the sum of $5,000 on the part of petitioner, a Negro citizen of the 48th precinct of Harris County, Texas, for the refusal of respondents, election and associate election judges respectively of that precinct, to give petitioner a ballot or to permit him to cast a ballot in the primary election of July 27, 1940, for the nomination of Democratic candidates for the Un ited States Senate and House of Representatives, and Governor and other state officers. The refusal is alleged to have been solely because of the race and color of the proposed voter.

* * * *

The State of Texas by its Constitution and statutes provides that every person, if certain other requirements are met which are not here in issue, qualified by residence in the district or county "shall be deemed a qualified elector.' (citation omitted) Primary elections for United States Senators, Congressmen and state officers are provided for by * * * the statutes. Under these [statutes], the Democratic Party was required to hold the primary which was the occasion of the alleged wrong to petitioner. * * * These nominations are to be made by the qualified voters of the party.

The Democratic Party of Texas is held by the Supreme Court of that state to be a "voluntary association,' (citation omitted) protected by Section 27 of the Bill of Rights, Art. 1, Constitution of Texas, from interference by the state except that:

"In the interest of fair methods and a fair expression by their members of their preferences in the selection of their nominees, the State may regulate such elections by proper laws.' (citation omitted) That court stated further:

"Since the right to organize and maintain a political party is one guaranteed by the Bill of Rights of this state, it necessarily follows that every privilege essential or reasonably appropriate to the exercise of that right is likewise guaranteed, including, of course, the privilege of determining the policies of the party and its membership. Without the privilege of determining the policy of a political association and its membership, the right to organize such an association would be a mere mockery. We think these rights, that is, the right to determine the membership of a political party and to determine its policies, of necessity are to be exercised by the State Convention of such party, and cannot, under any circumstances, be conferred upon a state or governmental agency.' (citation omitted)

The Democratic party on May 24, 1932, in a State Convention adopted the following resolution, which has not since been "amended, abrogated, annulled or avoided':

"Be it resolved that all white citizens of the State of Texas who are qualified to vote under the Constitution and laws of the State shall be eligible to membership in the Democratic party and, as such, entitled to participate in its deliberations.' It was by virtue of this resolution that the respondents refused to permit the petitioner to vote.

Texas is free to conduct her elections and limit her electorate as she may deem w ise, save only as her action may be affected by the prohibitions of the United States Constitution or in conflict with powers delegated to and exercised by the National Government. The Fourteenth Amendment forbids a state from making or enforcing any law which abridges the privileges or immunities of citizens of the United States and the Fifteenth Amendment specifically interdicts any denial or abridgement by a state of the right of citizens to vote on account of color. Respondents appeared in the District Court and the Circuit Court of Appeals and defended on the ground that the Democratic party of Texas is a voluntary organization with members banded together for the purpose of selecting individuals of the group representing the common political beliefs as candidates in the general election. As such a voluntary organization, it was claimed, the Democratic party is free to select its own membership and limit to whites participation in the party primary. Such action, the answer asserted, does not violate the Fourteenth, Fifteenth or Seventeenth Amendment as officers of government cannot be chosen at primaries and the Amendments are applicable only to general elections where governmental officers are actually elected. Primaries, it is said, are political party affairs, handled by party not governmental officers. * * *

* * * *

It may now be taken as a postulate that the right to vote in such a primary for the nomination of candidates without discrimination by the State, like the right to vote in a general election, is a right secured by the Constitution. * * * By the terms of the Fifteenth Amendment that right may not be abridged by any state on account of race. Under our Constitution the great privilege of the ballot may not be denied a man by the State because of his color.

* * * *

We think that this statutory system for the selection of party nominees for inclusion on the general election ballot makes the party which is required to follow these legislative directions an agency of the state in so far as it determines the participants in a primary election. The party takes its character as a state agency from the duties imposed upon it by state statutes; the duties do not become matters of private law because they are performed by a political party. The plan of the Texas primary follows substantially that of Louisiana, with the exception that in Louisiana the state pays the cost of the primary while Texas assesses the cost against candidates. In numerous instances, the Texas statutes fix or limit the fees to be charged. Whether paid directly by the state or through state requirements, it is state action which compels. When primaries become a part of the machinery for choosing officials, state and national, as they have here, the same tests to determine the character of discrimination or abridgement should be applied to the primary as are applied to the general election. If the state requires a certain electoral procedure, prescribes a general election ballot made up of party nominees so chosen and limits the choice of the electorate in general elections for state offices, practically speaking, to those whose names appear on such a ballot, it endorses, adopts and enforces the discrimination against Negroes, practiced by a party entrusted by Texas law with the determination of the qualifications of participants in the primary. This is state action within the meaning of the Fifteenth Amendment.

The United States is a constitutional democracy. Its organic law grants to all citizens a right to participate in the choice of elected officials without restriction by any state because of race. This grant to the people of the opportunity for choice is not to be nulified by a state through casting its electoral process in a form which permits a private organization to practice racial discrimination in the election. Constitutional rights would be of little value if they could be thus indirectly denied.

The privilege of membership in a party may be no concern of a state. But when, as here, that privilege is also the essential qualification for voting in a primary to select nominees for a general election, the state makes the action of the party the action of the state. In reaching this conclusion we are not unmindful of the desirability of continuity of decision in constitutional questions. However, when convinced of former error, this Court has never felt constrained to follow precedent. In constitutional questions, where correction depends upon amendment and not upon legislative action this Court throughout its history has freely exercised its power to reexamine the basis of its constitutional decisions. This has long been accepted practice, and this practice has continued to this day. This is particularly true when the decision believed erroneous is the application of a constitutional principle rather than an interpretation of the Constitution to extract the principle itself. Here we are applying the well established principle of the Fifteenth Amendment, forbidding the abridgement by a state of a citizen's right to vote. * * *

Decision

Judgment reversed.

State of **SOUTH CAROLINA**
v.
Nicholas deB. **KATZENBACH**
383 U.S. 301, 86 S.Ct. 803, 15 L.Ed.2d 769.
Argued Jan. 17, 18, 1966.
Decided March 7, 1966.

Introduction

A voting rights case in which the Court held that Congress had acted correctly by passing the Voting Rights Act as a way to implement the Fifteenth Amendment guarantee of the right to vote to every citizen of the United States regardless of race, color, or previous condition of servitude.

WESTLAW Summary

Bill in equity for determination of the validity of selected provisions of the Voting Rights Act of 1965 and for an injunction against enforcement of its provisions by United States Attorney General. The Supreme Court held that the provisions of the Voting Rights Act of 1965 pertaining to the suspension of eligibility tests or devices, review of proposed alterations of voting qualifications and procedures, appointment of federal voting examiners, examination of applicants for registration, challenges to eligibility listings, termination of listing procedures, and enforcement proceedings in criminal contempt cases were appropriate means for carrying out Congress' constitutional responsibilities under the Fifteenth Amendment and were consonant with all other provisions of the Constitution.

Case Excerpts

Mr. Chief Justice WARREN delivered the opinion of the Court.

By leave of the Court, South Carolina has filed a bill of complaint, seeking a declaration that selected provisions of the Voting

Rights Act of 1965 violate the Federal Constitution, and asking for an injunction against enforcement of these provisions by the Attorney General.

* * * *

The Voting Rights Act was designed by Congress to banish the blight of racial discrimination in voting, which has infected the electoral process in parts of our country for nearly a century. The Act creates stringent new remedies for voting discrimination where it persists on a pervasive scale, and in addition the statute strengthens existing remedies for pockets of voting discrimination elsewhere in the country. Congress assumed the power to prescribe these remedies from s 2 of the Fifteenth Amendment, which authorizes the National Legislature to effectuate by "appropriate' measures the constitutional prohibition against racial discrimination in voting. We hold that the sections of the Act which are properly before us are an appropriate means for carrying out Congress' constitutional responsibilities and are consonant with all other provisions of the Constitution. We therefore deny South Carolina's request that enforcement of these sections of the Act be enjoined.

* * * *

Despite the earnest efforts of the Justice Department and of many federal judges, these new laws have done little to cure the problem of voting discrimination. According to estimates by the Attorney General during hearings on the Act, registration of voting-age Negroes in Alabama rose only from 14.2% to 19.4% between 1958 and 1964; in Louisiana it barely inched ahead from 31.7% to 31.8% between 1956 and 1965; and in Mississippi it increased only from 4.4% to 6.4% between 1954 and 1964. In each instance, registration of voting-age whites ran roughly 50 percentage points or more ahead of Negro registration.

* * * *

The Voting Rights Act of 1965 reflects Congress' firm intention to rid the country of racial discrimination in voting. The heart of the Act is a complex scheme of stringent remedies aimed at areas where voting discrimination has been most flagrant.

* * * *

The remedial sections of the Act assailed by South Carolina automatically apply to any State, or to any separate political subdivision such as a county or parish, for which two findings have been made: (1) the Attorney General has determined that on November 1, 1964, it maintained a "test or device,' and (2) the Director of the Census has determined that less than 50% of its voting age residents were registered on November 1, 1964, or voted in the presidential election of November 1964.

* * * *

These provisions of the Voting Rights Act of 1965 are challenged on the fundamental ground that they exceed the powers of Congress and encroach on an area reserved to the States by the Constitution. * * *

* * * The language and purpose of the Fifteenth Amendment, the prior decisions construing its several provisions, and the general doctrines of constitutional interpretation, all point to one fundamental principle. As against the reserved powers of the States, Congress may use any rational means to effectuate the constitutional prohibition of racial discrimination in voting. * * *

Section 1 of the Fifteenth Amendment declares that "(t)he right of citizens of the United States to vote shall not be denied or abridged by the United States or by any State on account of race, color, or previous condition of servitude.' This declaration has always been treated as self-executing and has repeatedly been construed, without further legislative specification, to invalidate state voting qualifications or procedures which are discriminatory on their face or in practice. * * * The gist of the matter is that the Fifteenth Amendment supersedes contrary exertions of state power. "When a State exercises power wholly within the domain of state interest, it is insulated from federal judicial review. But such insulation is not carried over when state power is used as an instrument for circumventing a federally protected right.' (citation omitted)

South Carolina contends that the cases cited above are precedents only for the authority of the judiciary to strike down state statutes and procedures-that to allow an exercise of this authority by Congress would be to rob the courts of their rightful constitutional role. On the contrary, s 2 of the Fifteenth Amendment expressly declares that "Congress shall have power to enforce this article by appropriate legislation.' By adding this authorization, the Framers indicated that Congress was to be chiefly responsible for implementing the rights created in s 1. "It is the power of Congress which has been enlarged. Congress is authorized to enforce the prohibitions by appropriate legislation Some legislation is contemplated to make the (Civil War) amendments fully effective.' (citation omitted) Accordingly, in addition to the courts, Congress has full remedial powers to effectuate the constitutional prohibition against racial discrimination in voting.

Congress has repeatedly exercised these powers in the past, and its enactments have repeatedly been upheld. * * * On the rare occasions when the Court has found an unconstitutional exercise of these powers, in its opinion Congress had attacked evils not comprehended by the Fifteenth Amendment. * * *

* * * We therefore reject South Carolina's argument that Congress may appropriately do no more than to forbid violations of the Fifteenth Amendment in general terms-that the task of fashioning specific remedies or of applying them to particular localities must necessarily be left entirely to the courts. Congress is not circumscribed by any such artificial rules under s 2 of the Fifteenth Amendment. In the oft-repeated words of Chief Justice Marshall, referring to another specific legislative authorization in the Constitution, "This power, like all others vested in Congress, is complete in itself, may be exercised to its utmost extent, and acknowledges no limitations, other than are prescribed in the constitution.' (citation omitted)

* * * *

The Act suspends literacy tests and similar devices for a period of five years from the last occurrence of substantial voting discrimination. This was a legitimate response to the problem, for which there is ample precedent in Fifteenth Amendment cases. Ibid. Underlying the response was the feeling that States and political subdivisions which had been allowing white illiterates to vote for years could not sincerely complain about "dilution' of their electorates through the registration of Negro illiterates. Congress knew that continuance of the tests and devices in use at the present time, no matter how fairly administered in the future, would freeze the effect of past discrimination in favor of unqualified white registrants. Congress permissibly rejected the alternative of requiring a complete re-registration of all voters, believing that this would be too harsh on many whites who had enjoyed the franchise for their entire adult lives.

* * * *

The Act suspends new voting regulations pending scrutiny by federal authorities to determine whether their use would violate the Fifteenth Amendment. This may have been an uncommon exercise of congressional power, as South Carolina contends, but the Court has recognized that exceptional conditions can justify legislative measures not otherwise appropriate.

* * * *

The Act authorizes the appointment of federal examiners to list qualified applicants who are thereafter entitled to vote, subject to an expeditious challenge procedure. * * *

* * * *

After enduring nearly a century of widespread resistance to the Fifteenth Amendment, Congress has marshalled an array of potent weapons against the evil, with authority in the Attorney General to employ them effectively. Many of the areas directly affected by this development have indicated their willingness to abide by any restraints legitimately imposed upon them. We here hold that the portions of the Voting Rights Act properly before us are a valid means for carrying out the commands of the Fifteenth Amendment. Hopefully, millions of non-white Americans will now be able to participate for the first time on an equal basis in the government under which they live. We may finally look forward to the day when truly "(t)he right of citizens of the United States to vote shall not be denied or abridged by the United States or by any State on account of race, color, or previous condition of servitude.'

Decision

Bill dismissed.

UNITED STATES
v.
Richard M. **NIXON**, et al.
418 U.S. 683, 94 S.Ct. 3090, 41 L.Ed.2d 1039
Argued July 8, 1974.
Decided July 24, 1974.

Introduction

A presidential executive privilege case in which the Court ruled that President Nixon had to hand over secret tapes containing his Oval Office conversations while in the White House. The Court ruled that executive privilege could not be used to prevent evidence from being heard in criminal proceedings.

WESTLAW Summary

Prosecution of former government officials and presidential campaign officials for conspiracy to defraud the United States and to obstruct justice, and for other offenses, wherein the special prosecutor caused a third-party subpoena duces tecum to be issued directing the President to produce tape recordings and documents relating to conversations with aides and advisors. The United States District Court for the District of Columbia, denied the President's motion to quash subpoena and an appeal was taken. Certiorari before judgment was granted to bring the matter before the Supreme Court before disposition by the Court of Appeals. The Supreme Court held that the dispute was justiciable; that the District Court was not shown to have erred in determining that the special prosecutor's showing of relevancy, admissibility, and specificity was sufficient to warrant the issuance of the order; and that the President's generalized interest in confidentiality, unsupported by a claim of need to protect military, diplomatic, or sensitive national security secrets, could not prevail against the special prosecutor's demonstrated, specific need for the tape recordings and documents.

Case Excerpts

Mr. Chief Justice BURGER delivered the opinion of the Court.

This litigation presents for review the denial of a motion, filed in the District Court on behalf of the President of the United States * * * to quash a third-party subpoena duces tecum issued by the United States District Court for the District of Columbia. The subpoena directed the President to produce certain tape recordings and documents relating to his conversations with aides and advisers. The court rejected the President's claims of absolute executive privilege, of lack of jurisdiction, and of failure to satisfy the requirements of Rule 17(c). The President appealed to the Court of Appeals. We granted both the United States' petition for certiorari before judgment and also the President's cross-petition for certiorari before judgment because of the public importance of the issues presented and the need for their prompt resolution

On March 1, 1974, a grand jury of the United States District Court for the District of Columbia returned an indictment charging seven named individuals with various offenses, including conspiracy to defraud the United States and to obstruct justice. Although he was not designated as such in the indictment, the grand jury named the President, among others, as an unindicted coconspirator. On April 18, 1974, upon motion of the Special Prosecutor, a subpoena duces tecum was issued pursuant to Rule 17(c) to the President by the United States District Court and made returnable on May 2, 1974. This subpoena required the production, in advance of the September 9 trial date, of certain tapes, memoranda, papers, transcripts or other writings relating to certain precisely identified meetings between the President and others. * * * On April 30, the President publicly released edited transcripts of 43 conversations; portions of 20 conversations subject to subpoena in the present case were included. On May 1, 1974, the President's counsel, filed a "special appearance' and a motion to quash the subpoena under Rule 17(c). This motion was accompanied by a formal claim of privilege. At a subsequent hearing, further motions to expunge the grand jury's action naming the President as an unindicted coconspirator and for protective orders against the disclosure of that information were filed or raised orally by counsel for the President.

On May 20, 1974, the District Court denied the motion to quash and the motions to expunge and for protective orders. It further ordered "the President or any subordinate officer, official, or employee with custody or control of the documents or objects subpoenaed,' to deliver to the District Court, on or before May 31, 1974, the originals of all subpoenaed items, as well as an index and analysis of those items, together with tape copies of those portions of the subpoenaed recordings for which transcripts had been released to the public by the President on April 30. The District Court rejected jurisdictional challenges based on a contention that the dispute was nonjusticiable because it was between the Special Prosecutor and the Chief Executive and hence "intra-executive' in character; it also rejected the contention that the Judiciary was without authority to review an assertion of executive privilege by the President. * * *

The District Court held that the judiciary, not the President, was the final arbiter of a claim of executive privilege. The court concluded that under the circumstances of this case the presumptive privilege was overcome by the Special Prosecutor's prima facie "demonstration of need sufficiently compelling to warrant judicial examination in chambers . . . .' * * *

* * * *

In the performance of assigned constitutional duties each branch of the Government must initially interpret the Constitution, and the interpretation of its powers by any branch is due great respect from the others. The President's counsel, as we have noted, reads the Constitution as providing an absolute privilege of confidentiality for all Presidential communications. Many decisions of this Court, however, have unequivocally reaffirmed the holding of Marbury v. Madison that "(i)t is emphatically the province and duty of the jud icial department to say what the law is.' (citation omitted)

No holding of the Court has defined the scope of judicial power specifically relating to the enforcement of a subpoena for confidential Presidential communications for use in a criminal prosecution, but other exercises of power by the Executive Branch and the Legislative Branch have been found invalid as in conflict with the Constitution. * * * Since this Court has consistently exercised the power to construe and delineate claims arising under express powers, it must follow that the Court has authority to interpret claims with respect to powers alleged to derive from enumerated powers.

* * * *

Notwithstanding the deference each branch must accord the others, the "judicial Power of the United States' vested in the federal courts by Art. III, s 1, of the Constitution can no more be shared with the Executive Branch than the Chief Executive, for example, can share with the Judiciary the veto power, or the Congress share with the Judiciary the power to override a Presidential veto. Any other conclusion would be contrary to the basic concept of separation of powers and the checks and balances that flow from the scheme of a tripartite government. We therefore reaffirm that it is the province and duty of this Court "to say what the law is' with respect to the claim of privilege presented in this case. (citation omitted)

In support of his claim of absolute privilege, the President's counsel urges two grounds, one of which is common to all governments and one of which is peculiar to our system of separation of powers. The first ground is the valid need for protection of communications between high Government officials and those who advise and assist them in the performance of their manifold duties; the importance of this confidentiality is too plain to require further discussion. Human experience teaches that those who expect public dissemination of their remarks may well temper candor with a concern for appearances and for their own interests to the detriment of the decisionmaking process. Whatever the nature of the privilege of confidentiality of Presidential communications in the exercise of Art. II powers, the privilege can be said to derive from the supremacy of each branch within its own assigned area of constitutional duties. Certain powers and privileges flow from the nature of enumerated powers; the protection of the confidentiality of Presidential communications has similar constitutional underpinnings.

The second ground asserted by the President's counsel in support of the claim of absolute privilege rests on the doctrine of separation of powers. Here it is argued that the independence of the Executive Branch within its own sphere insulates a President from a judicial subpoena in an ongoing criminal prosecution, and thereby protects confidential Presidential communications.

However, neither the doctrine of separation of powers, nor the need for confidentiality of high-level communications, without more, can sustain an absolute, unqualified Presidential privilege of immunity from judicial process under all circumstances. The President's need for complete candor and objectivity from advisers calls for great deference from the courts. However, when the privilege depends solely on the broad, undifferentiated claim of public interest in the confidentiality of such conversations, a confrontation with other values arises. Absent a claim of need to protect military, diplomatic, or sensitive national security secrets, we find it difficult to accept the argument that even the very important interest in confidentiality of Presidential communications is significantly diminished by production of such material for in camera inspection with all the protection that a district court will be obliged to provide.

The impediment that an absolute, unqualified privilege would place in the way of the primary constitutional duty of the Judicial Branch to do justice in criminal prosecutions would plainly conflict with the function of the courts under Art. III. In designing the structure of our Government and dividing and allocating the sovereign power among three co-equal branches, the Framers of the Constitution sought to provide a comprehensive system, but the separate powers were not intended to operate with absolute independence.

* * * *

Since we conclude that the legitimate needs of the judicial process may outweigh Presidential privilege, it is necessary to resolve those competing interests in a manner that preserves the essential functions of each branch. The right and indeed the duty to resolve that question does not free the Judiciary from according high respect to the representations made on behalf of the President.

The expectation of a President to the confidentiality of his conversations and correspondence, like the claim of confidentiality of judicial deliberations, for example, has all the values to which we accord deference for the privacy of all citizens and, added to those values, is the necessity for protection of the public interest in candid, objective, and even blunt or harsh opinions in Presidential decisionmaking. A President and those who assist him must be free to explore alternatives in the process of shaping policies and making decisions and to do so in a way many would be unwilling to express except privately. These are the considerations justifying a presumptive privilege for Presidential communications. The privilege is fundamental to the operation of Government and inextricably rooted in the separation of powers under the Constitution. * * *

But this presumptive privilege must be considered in light of our historic commitment to the rule of law. * * * The very integrity of the judicial system and public confidence in the system depend on full disclosure of all the facts, within the framework of the rules of evidence. To ensure that justice is done, it is imperative to the function of courts that compulsory process be available for the production of evidence needed either by the prosecution or by the defense.

* * * *

* * * Nowhere in the Constitution, as we have noted earlier, is there any explicit reference to a privilege of confidentiality, yet to the extent this interest relates to the effective discharge of a President's powers, it is constitutionally based.

* * * *

We conclude that when the ground for asserting privilege as to subpoenaed materials sought for use in a criminal trial is based only on the generalized interest in confidentiality, it cannot prevail over the fundamental demands of due process of law in the fair administration of criminal justice. The generalized assertion of privilege must yield to the demonstrated, specific need for evidence in a pending criminal trial.

* * * Since this matter came before the Court during the pendency of a criminal prosecution, and on representations that time is of the essence, the mandate shall issue forthwith.

Decision

Affirmed.

Frederick **WALZ**
v.
NEW YORK CITY TAX COMMISSION.
397 U.S. 664, 90 S.Ct. 1409, 25 L.Ed.2d 697
Argued Nov. 19, 1969.
Decided May 4, 1970.

Introduction

A separation of church and state case in which the Court ruled that tax exemptions for churches do not violate the First Amendment, but rather show the state's "benevolent neutrality" toward religion.

WESTLAW Summary

Realty owner sought injunction to prevent New York City Tax Commission from granting property tax exemptions to religious organizations for properties used solely for religious worship. The Supreme Court of New York, Appellate Division, affirmed an order of the Supreme Court, Special Term, denying the motion by plaintiff for summary judgment and granting the cross motion for summary judgment dismissing the complaint. Plaintiff appealed on constitutional grounds. The Court of Appeals of New York affirmed and the plaintiff appealed. The Supreme Court held that New York statute exempting from real property taxes realty owned by an association organized exclusively for religious purposes and used exclusively for carrying out such purposes is not unconstitutional as an attempt to establish, sponsor or support religion or as an interference with free exercise of religion.

Case Excerpts

Mr. Chief Justice BURGER delivered the opinion of the Court.

Appellant, the owner of real estate in Richmond County, New York, sought an injunction in the New York courts to prevent the New York City Tax Commission from granting property tax exemptions to religious organizations for religious properties used solely for religious worship. The exemption from state taxes is authorized by Art. 16, s 1, of the New York Constitution, which provides in relevant part:

"Exemptions from taxation may be granted only by general laws. Exemptions may be altered or repealed except those exempting real or personal property used exclusively for religious, educational or charitable purposes as defined by law and owned by any corporation or association organized or conducted exclusively for one or more of such purposes and not operating for profit.'

The essence of appellant's contention was that the New York City Tax Commission's grant of an exemption to church property indirectly requires the appellant to make a contribution to religious bodies and thereby violates provisions prohibiting the establishment of religion under the First Amendment which, under the Fourteenth Amendment, is binding on the States.

* * * *

The Establishment and Free Exercise Clauses of the First Amendment are not the most precisely drawn portions of the Constitution. The sweep of the absolute prohibitions in the Religion Clauses may have been calculated; but the purpose was to state an objective not to write a statute. In attempting to articulate the scope of the two Religion Clauses, the Court's opinions reflect the limitations inherent in formulating general principles on a case-by-case basis. The considerable internal inconsistency in the opinions of the Court derives from what, in retrospect, may have been to sweeping utterances on aspects of these clauses that seemed clear in relation to the particular cases but have limited meaning as general principles.

* * * *

* * * The general principle deducible from the First Amendment and all that has been said by the Court is this: that we will not tolerate either governmentally established religion or governmental interference with religion. Short of those expressly proscribed governmental acts there is room for play in the joints productive of a benevolent neutrality which will permit religious exercise to exist without sponsorship and without interference.

Each value judgment under the Religion Clauses must therefore turn on whether particular acts in question are intended to establish or interfere with religious beliefs and practices or have the effect of doing so. Adherence to the policy of neutrality that derives from an accommodation of the Establishment and Free Exercise Clauses has prevented the kind of involvement that would tip the balance toward government control of churches or governmental restraint on religious practice.

Adherents of particular faiths and individual churches frequently take strong positions on public issues including, as this case reveals in the several briefs amici, vigorous advocacy of legal or constitutional positions. Of course, churches as much as secular bodies and private citizens have that right. No perfect or absolute separation is really possible; the very existence of the Religion Clauses is an involvement of sorts-one that seeks to mark boundaries to avoid excessive entanglement.

* * * *

The legislative purpose of a property tax exemption is neither the advancement nor the inhibition of religion; it is neither sponsorship nor hostility. New York, in common with the other States, has determined that certain entities that exist in a harmonious relationshi p to the community at large, and that foster its "moral or mental improvement,' should not be inhibited in their activities by property taxation or the hazard of loss of those properties for nonpayment of taxes. It has not singled out one particular church or religious group or even churches as such; rather, it has granted exemption to all houses of religious worship within a broad class of property owned by nonprofit, quasi-public corporations which include hospitals, libraries, playgrounds, scientific, professional, historical, and patriotic groups. The State has an affirmative policy that considers these groups as beneficial and stabilizing influences in community life and finds this classification useful, desirable, and in the public interest. Qualification for tax exemption is not perpetual or immutable; some tax-exempt groups lose that status when their activities take them outside the classification and new entities can come into being and qualify for exemption.

* * * *

The grant of a tax exemption is not sponsorship since the government does not transfer part of its revenue to churches but simply abstains from demanding that the church support the state. No one has ever suggested that tax exemption has converted libraries, art galleries, or hospitals into arms of the state or put employees "on the public payroll.' There is no genuine nexus between tax exemption and establishment of religion. * * * The exemption creates only a minimal and remote involvement between church and state and far less than taxation of churches. It restricts the fiscal relationship between church and state, and tends to complement and reinforce the desired separation insulating each from the other.

Separation in this context cannot mean absence of all contact; the complexities of modern life inevitably produce some contact and the fire and police protection received by houses of religious worship are no more than incidental benefits accorded all persons or institutions within a State's boundaries, along with many other exempt organizations. The appellant has not established even an arguable quantitative correlation between the payment of an ad valorem property tax and the receipt of these municipal benefits.

* * * *

It appears that at least up to 1885 this Court, reflecting more than a century of our history and uninterrupted practice, accepted without discussion the proposition that federal or state grants of tax exemption to churches were not a violation of the Religion Clauses of the First Amendment. As to the New York statute, we now confirm that view.

Decision

Affirmed.

James P. **WESBERRY**, Jr., et al.,
v.
Carl E. **SANDERS**, et al.
376 U.S. 1, 84 S.Ct. 526, 11 L.Ed.2d 481.
Argued Nov. 18 and 19, 1963.
Decided Feb. 17, 1964.

Introduction

A Fourteenth Amendment/Congressional districting case in which the Court ruled that the state of Georgia's formation of Congressional districts created such huge population differences that they violated the Constitution. This case was the basis of the Court's ruling later requiring one-person, one vote.

WESTLAW Summary

Action, in the United States District Court for the Northern District of Georgia, by qualified voters to strike down a Georgia statute prescribing congressional districts. The three-judge District Court dismissed the complaint, and plaintiffs appealed. The Su preme Court held that the complaint presented a justiciable controversy, and that the apportionment of congressional districts so that single congressman represented from two to three times as many Fifth District voters as were represented by each of the congressmen from the other Georgia districts grossly discriminated against voters in the Fifth District in violation of the constitutional requirement that representatives be chosen by people of the several states.

Case Excerpts

Mr. Justice BLACK delivered the opinion of the Court.

Appellants are citizens and qualified voters of Fulton County, Georgia, and as such are entitled to vote in congressional elections in Georgia's Fifth Congressional District. That district, one of ten created by a 1931 Georgia statute, includes Fulton, DeKalb, and Rockdale

Counties and has a population according to the 1960 census of 823,680. The average population of the ten districts is 394,312, less than half that of the Fifth. One district, the Ninth, has only 272,154 people, less than one-third as many as the Fifth. Since there is only one Congressman for each district, this inequality of population means that the Fifth District's Congressman has to represent from two to three times as many people as do Congressmen from some of the other Georgia districts.

Claiming that these population disparities deprived them and voters similarly situated of a right under the Federal Constitution to have their votes for Congressmen given the same weight as the votes of other Georgians, the appellants brought this action asking that the Georgia statute be declared invalid and that the appellees, the Governor and Secretary of State of Georgia, be enjoined from conducting elections under it. * * *

* * * We agree with the District Court that the 1931 Georgia apportionment grossly discriminates against voters in the Fifth Congressional District. A single Congressman represents from two to three times as many Fifth District voters as are represented by each of the Congressmen from the other Georgia congressional districts. The apportionment statute thus contracts the value of some votes and expands that of others. If the Federal Constitution intends that when qualified voters elect members of Congress each vote be given as much weight as any other vote, then this statute cannot stand.

* * * *

It would defeat the principle solemnly embodied in the Great Compromise-equal representation in the House for equal numbers of people-for us to hold that, within the States, legislatures may draw the lines of congressional districts in such a way as to give some voters a greater voice in choosing a Congressman than others. The House of Represenatives, the Convention agreed, was to represent the people as individuals, and on a basis of complete equality for each voter. * * *

* * * *

It is in the light of such history that we must construe Art. I, s 2, of the Constitution, which, carrying out the ideas of Madison and those of like views, provides that Representatives shall be chosen "by the People of the several States' and shall be "apportioned among the several States * * * according to their respective Numbers.' It is not surprising that our Court has held that this Article gives persons qualified to vote a constitutional right to vote and to have their votes counted. (citations omitted) No right is more precious in a free country than that of having a voice in the election of those who make the laws under which, as good citizens, we must live. Other rights, even the most basic, are illusory if the right to vote is undermined. Our Constitution leaves no room for classification of people in a way that unnecessarily abridges this right. * * *

* * * *

While it may not be possible to draw congressional districts with mathematical precision, that is no excuse for ignoring our Constitution's plain objective of making equal representation for equal numbers of people the fundamental goal for the House of Representatives. That is the high standard of justice and common sense which the Founders set for us.

Decision

Reversed and remanded.

ZORACH, et al.
v.
CLAUSON, et al.
343 U.S. 306, 72 S.Ct. 679, 96 L.Ed. 954
Argued Jan. 31 and Feb. 1, 1952.
Decided April 28, 1952.

Introduction

A "release time" case in which the Court upheld New York City's program because that program required religious classes to be held in private places and not on school campuses.

WESTLAW Summary

Tessim Zorach and another brought a proceeding for review of the action of Andrew G. Clauson, Jr., and others, constituting The Board of Education of the City of New York, in establishing a "released time' program for the religious instruction of public school children. The Special Term entered an order favoring defendants, and petitioners appealed. From an order of the Appellate Division likewise favoring defendants, petitioners again appealed. The New York Court of Appeals affirmed the Appellate Division's order, and the petitioners appealed once again. The United States Supreme Court held that the statute providing for the release of public school pupils from school attendance to attend religious classes was constitutional.

Case Excerpts

Mr. Justice DOUGLAS delivered the opinion of the Court.

New York City has a program which permits its public schools to release students during the school day so that they may leave the school buildings and school grounds and go to religious centers for religious instruction or devotional exercises. A student is released on written request of his parents. Those not released stay in the classrooms. The churches make weekly reports to the schools, sending a list of children who have been released from public school but who have not reported for religious instruction.

This "released time' program involves neither religious instruction in public school classrooms nor the expenditure of public funds. All costs, including the application blanks, are paid by the religious organizations. * * *

Appellants, who are taxpayers and residents of New York City and whose children attend its public schools challenge the present law * * *. Their argument, stated elaborately in various ways, reduces itself to this: the weight and influence of the school is put behind a program for religious instruction; public school teachers police it, keeping tab on students who are released; the classroom activities come to a halt while the students who are released for religious instruction are on leave; the school is a crutch on which the churches are leaning for support in their religious training; without the cooperation of the schools this "released time' program * * * would be futile and ineffective. The New York Court of Appeals sustained the law against this claim of unconstitutionality. The case is here on appeal.

The briefs and arguments are replete with data bearing on the merits of this type of "released time' program. Views pro and con are expressed, based on practical experience with these programs and with their implications. We do not stop to summarize these materials nor to burden the opinion with an analysis of them. For they involve considerations not germane to the narrow constitutional issue presented. They largely concern the wisdom of the system, its efficiency from an educational point of view, and the political considerations which have motivated its adoption or rejection in some communities. Those matters are of no concern here, since our problem reduces itself to whether New York by this system has either prohibited the "free exercise' of religion or has made a law "respecting an establishment of religion' within the meaning of the First Amendment.

It takes obtuse reasoning to inject any issue of the "free exercise' of religion into the present case. No one is forced to go to the religious classroom and no religious exercise or instruction is brought to the classrooms of the public schools. A student need not take religious instruction. He is left to his own desires as to the manner or time of his religious devotions, if any.

There is a suggestion that the system involves the use of coercion to get public school students into religious classrooms. There is no evidence in the record before us that supports that conclusion. The present record indeed tells us that the school authorities are neutral in this regard and do no more than release students whose parents so request. If in fact coercion were used, if it were established that any one or more teachers were using their office to persuade or force students to take the religious instruction, a wholly different case would be presented. Hence we put aside that claim of coercion both as respects the "free exercise' of religion and "an establishment of religion' within the meaning of the First Amendment.

Moreover, apart from that claim of coercion, we do not see how New York by this type of "released time' program has made a law respecting an establishment of religion within the meaning of the First Amendment. There is much talk of the separation of Church and State in the history of the Bill of Rights and in the decisions clustering around the First Amendment. There cannot be the slightest doubt that the First Amendment reflects the philosophy that Church and State should be separated. And so far as interference with the "free exercise' of religion and an "establishment' of religion are concerned, the separation must be complete and unequivocal. The First Amendment within the scope of its coverage permits no exception; the prohibition is absolute. The First Amendment, however, does not say that in every and all respects there shall be a separation of Church and State. Rather, it studiously defines the manner, the specific ways, in which there shall be no concert or union or dependency one on the other. That is the common sense of the matter. Otherwise the state and religion would be aliens to each other-hostile, suspicious, and even unfriendly. Churches could not be required to pay even property taxes. Municipalities would not be permitted to render police or fire protection to religious groups. Policemen who helped parishioners into their places of worship would violate the Constitution. Prayers in our legislative halls; the appeals to the Almighty in the messages of the Chief Executive; the proclamations making Thanksgiving Day a holiday; "so help me God' in our courtroom oaths-these and all other references to the Almighty that run through our laws, our public rituals, our ceremonies would be flouting the First Amendment. A fastidious atheist or agnostic could even object to the supplication with which the Court opens each session: "God save the United States and this Honorable Court.'

We would have to press the concept of separation of Church and State to these extremes to condemn the present law on constitutional grounds. The nullification of this law would have wide and profound effects. A catholic student applies to his teacher for permission to leave the school during hours on a Holy Day of Obligation to attend a mass. A Jewish student asks his teacher for permission to be excused for Yom Kippur. A Protestant wants the afternoon off for a family baptismal ceremony. In each case the teacher requires parental consent in writing. In each case the teacher, in order to make sure the student is not a truant, goes further and requires a report from the priest, the rabbi, or the minister. The teacher in other words cooperates in a religious program to the extent of making it possible for her students to participate in it. Whether she does it occasionally for a few students, regularly for one, or pursuant to a systematized program designed to further the religious needs of all the students does not alter the character of the act.

We are a religious people whose institutions presuppose a Supreme Being. We guarantee the freedom to worship as one chooses. We make room for as wide a variety of beliefs and creeds as the spiritual needs of man deem necessary. We sponsor an attitude on the part of government that shows no partiality to any one group and that lets each flourish according to the zeal of its adherents and the appeal of its dogma. When the state encourages religious instruction or cooperates with religious authorities by adjusting the schedule of public events to sectarian needs, it follows the best of our traditions. For it then respects the religious nature of our people and accommodates the public service to their spiritual needs. To hold that it may not would be to find in the Constitution a requirement that the government show a callous indifference to religious groups. That would be preferring those who believe in no religion over those who do believe. Government may not finance religious groups nor undertake religious instruction nor blend secular and sectarian education nor use secular institutions to force one or some religion on any person. But we find no constitutional requirement which makes it necessary for government to be hostile to religion and to throw its weight against efforts to widen the effective scope of religious influence. The government must be neutral when it comes to competition between sects. It may not thrust any sect on any person. It may not make a religious observance compulsory. It may not coerce anyone to attend church, to observe a religious holiday, or to take religious instruction. But it can close its doors or suspend its operations as to those who want to repair to their religious sanctuary for worship or instruction. No more than that is undertaken here.

This program may be unwise and improvident from an educational or a community viewpoint. That appeal is made to us on a theory, previously advanced, that each case must be decided on the basis of "our own prepossessions.' (citation omitted) Our individual preferences, however, are not the constitutional standard. The constitutional standard is the separation of Church and State. The problem, like many problems in constitutional law, is one of degree. * * *

* * * Here, as we have said, the public schools do no more than accommodate their schedules to a program of outside religious instruction. * * * [The] present released time program [is lawful] unless separation of Church and State means that public institutions can make no adjustments of their schedules to accommodate the religious needs of the people. We cannot read into the Bill of Rights such a philosophy of hostility to religion.

Decision

Affirmed.

Notes

Notes

Notes